The Certainty of Uncertainty

For Heinz von Foerster

The Certainty
of Uncertainty

Dialogues Introducing Constructivism

Bernhard Poerksen

Translated by Alison Rosemary Koeck
and Wolfram Karl Koeck

IMPRINT ACADEMIC

Copyright © Bernhard Poerksen, 2004

The moral rights of the author has been asserted
No part of any contribution may be reproduced in any form
without permission, except for the quotation of brief passages
in criticism and discussion.

The German original was first published under the title:
Bernhard Pörksen, *Die Gewissheit der Ungewissheit. Gespräche zum
Konstruktivismus*, Heidelberg: Carl-Auer-Systeme 2001

English translation by Alison Rosemary Koeck
and Wolfram Karl Koeck

Published in the UK by Imprint Academic
PO Box 200, Exeter EX5 5YX, UK

Published in the USA by Imprint Academic
Philosophy Documentation Center
PO Box 7147, Charlottesville, VA 22906-7147, USA

ISBN 0 907845 819

A CIP catalogue record for this book is available from the
British Library and US Library of Congress

www.imprint-academic.com

Contents

Acknowledgments vi

Preface vii

1 **At each and every moment I can decide who I am** 1
Heinz von Foerster on the observer, on dialogical living,
and on a constructivist philosophy of distinctions

2 **We can never know what goes on in somebody else's head** . 25
Ernst von Glasersfeld on truth and viability, language and
knowledge, and the premises of constructivist education

3 **The knowledge of knowledge entails responsibility** 47
Humberto R. Maturana on truth and oppression, structure
determinism and dictatorship, and the autopoiesis of living

4 **Truth is what works** 85
Francisco J. Varela on cognitive science, Buddhism, the
inseparability of subject and object, and the exaggerations
of constructivism

5 **We are constructs ourselves** 109
Gerhard Roth on the creation of reality in the brain, on a
reality independent from human consciousness, and on the
relationship between neurobiology and philosophy

6 **We can never start from scratch** 133
Siegfried J. Schmidt on individuals and society, on the
reality of the media, and on the constructivist conception
of empirical knowledge

7 **The freedom to venture into the unknown** 153
Helm Stierlin on guilt and responsibility in systemic and
constructivist thought, on the dialectical nature of human
relations, and on the ethos of the therapist

8 **Reality: we can only know what it is *not*** 173
Paul Watzlawick on the axioms of communication,
on the hidden realism of psychiatric diagnoses, and on
the constructivist vision of human existence

Biographical note on the author 192

Acknowledgements

My thanks are due first to all those who were willing to grant me hours of their time, often for several days, in the most diverse places of the world, for the conversations that are reproduced in this book. They generously gave their time to a person who was usually unknown to them and who could present no particular academic decorations to sanction his undertaking; and they carefully authorised the resulting interviews. (Possible misinterpretations, which may have sneaked in through section titles and brief characterisations in the biographical sketches, are to be charged entirely to my account.) I have to thank Julia Raabe for the competent comments she offered on the first transcriptions of the conversations: her fearless application of red ink improved the manuscript considerably. I dedicate the book to the dialogist, teacher, and friend, Heinz von Foerster. Without his encouragement and support, this book would never have materialised.

The circular view
of the world

When the latest research report of the Biological Computer Laboratory was published on 1 November 1970, nobody could possibly have foreseen the repercussions of the ideas it contained. The essay of about 70 pages, entitled *Biology of Cognition*, represented a new departure in the history of philosophy and a central document for the school of thought that is known as constructivism today. Its author, the Chilean biologist Humberto R. Maturana, who was working in the USA at the time, in vigorous language pleads for the study of the processes of cognition from a biological perspective. Epistemology, the theory of knowledge — once a central domain of philosophy — is turned into a scientific discipline. It investigates thinking and perceiving by means of experiments and empirical procedures, and it completes this change of role both in self-presentation and methodology: the reflecting philosopher as the experimenter in the laboratory. Humberto R. Maturana unequivocally points out that all those seeking to probe the truth of what we perceive with the eyes of a biologist, will inevitably have to accept that they are themselves among the objects they want to describe. They are living systems that want to understand living systems. Human subjects study objects that are identical with themselves. The situation turns circular as perceivers struggle to understand the processes of perceiving. We are reminded of the mythological figure of the Ouroboros: the snake eating its own tail; a brain explaining the brain; human knowers striving to understand understanding. Human subjects turn into their own objects.

Humberto R. Maturana's essay, after only a few pages, comes up with a conclusion and a central statement that illuminates the basic tenets of constructivism, and thus the topic of this book, which is meant to be an introduction to this mode of thought in the form of interviews. His statement, at first glance, appears to be a triviality; on closer inspection, however, it discloses a different view of the world. It simply says: "Anything said is said by an observer." (Maturana 1979, p. 8) It is of crucial importance that the existence of an external reality is not denied here; that this is not a statement of solipsism declaring everything a chimera and figment of the individual mind. Nor can the author be suspected of being a naive realist. He does not believe in the observer-independent existence of objects that are — in an ontologically congruent way — mirrored in the human knower's mind. Maturana's views, and the constructivists' views in general, represent a middle course between the varieties of realism and the exaggerations of solipsism. Neither Maturana nor the other founding figures of the constructivist school of thought, which deals with the origin and creation of conceptions of reality, deny the existence of an external world; they all deny, however, that it is possible to know that external world in a subject-independent way. Every act of cognition, it is claimed, necessarily rests on the constructions of observers — and not on the point-to-point correspondence of perception and external reality. "Anything said is said by an observer."

Referring all knowledge back to knowing subjects manoeuvres these knowing subjects into the centre and makes them the focal topic. The ontological perspective, which entices us to search for invariable ontic facts, changes into a fundamental epistemological quest. We may and must now query how and what observers observe — and perhaps we can hope to find the answers in experiments on colour perception and gestalt comprehension. We may possibly expect to discover them in processes of stimulus encoding, and we may then attempt to show that the human brain, which has no direct contact with its environment, derives its internal perceptual riches that we *experience* as a colourful external world, from quantities of indistinguishable grey noise supplied by external stimuli. In other contexts, however, it is claimed that *reality* cannot be explained by recourse to the biological constitution of humans; its development and creation must be essentially linked to social processes. It is, we hear, socially constructed and results from the dependence of human beings on groups and histories, on places and traditions. In this way, we could roam through disciplines and faculties — and everywhere encounter the millennium question of the observer. We come upon it in quantum physics and in systems theory, in the work of social psychologists and sociologists of knowledge, and we discover it in philosophy and cognitive science.

The discovery of the observer

However, the ominous figure of the observer, which seems to have become a stock in trade of any epistemological debate today, has not always been that prominent. It had to be uncovered and highlighted again by a number of cyberneticians, biologists, psychologists, and communication scientists — the originators of constructivism. They have provided key concepts for the international community of scientists, still relevant today, and they have managed to create an interdisciplinary forum for the critical discussion of crucial epistemological questions that has increasingly involved the general public. Their theses, concepts, and the possibilities of their application in management, education, and psychotherapy, are meanwhile debated even in the daily press. They are — following the order of the contributions to this volume — the physicist and cybernetician Heinz von Foerster, the psychologist Ernst von Glasersfeld, the biologists Humberto R. Maturana and Francisco J. Varela, the brain scientist Gerhard Roth, the communication scientist Siegfried J. Schmidt, the psychologists and family therapists Helm Stierlin and Paul Watzlawick. With their theories and models, stories and experiments, they have supplied new and epoch-specific arguments to substantiate the early epistemological doubts of the sceptics. They are united in their criticism of dogmatic positions of all forms and shapes, and they are precursors of an intellectual culture, which has removed the rigid barrier between the natural and the cultural sciences.

Still, despite everything the founding fathers of constructivism assembled here may have in common, there are naturally differences that divide them. Some of them describe the individual or even the individual brain as the relevant producer of reality; others base their conceptions on clearly larger-scale units like families, groups, societies, or cultures. These different approaches cannot easily be reconciled because they rest on barely compatible premises. The biologists, cognitive and brain scientists, on the one hand, concentrate their constructivist argument primarily on the individual. Their focus of interest is on the singular and autonomous observer. For the communication scientists and the family therapists of a systemic persuasion, on the other hand, the emphasis is not primarily on the cognitive autonomy of human individuals but on their patently obvious social orientation. In their view, reality arises within the framework of a society — and that means that all individuals must be seen as entities that are formed by their societies and their cultures. They observe with the eyes of their groups, they see the world against the background of their origins, and they cannot, therefore, be regarded as virtually blind black boxes or monads because they are, under all circumstances, open and extremely receptive to external impressions.

One common denominator of the constructivists voicing their opinions here is, consequently, the concentration on the observer. The observer is the point of fixation for all the divergent interests; the observer, by general consent, plays the central role in any cognitive process. Despite all the differences, such a common research interest is in itself of great consequence, of course, because it entails the need to re-assess the investigative efforts of one's own in relation to those of others. It is, in particular, the evaluation of the description of a hypothesised external world that changes: if knowledge is strictly tied to the individual knower, then descriptions are necessarily always also self-descriptions. They reveal the cognitive strengths and weaknesses, predilections and interests of those who see and perceive something. The biologist and communication scientist Francisco J. Varela, who has meanwhile turned into a critic of constructivism, writes in one of his early papers about this possibly somewhat puzzling view of observation with great precision: "In finding the world as we do, we forget all we did to find it as such, and when we are reminded of it in retracing our steps back to indication, we find little more than a mirror-to-mirror image of ourselves and the world. In contrast with what is commonly assumed, a description, when carefully inspected, reveals the properties of the observer." (Varela 1975, p. 22) Such a view of things leads to the unpleasant realisation that our craving for certainty and truth is shattered. The claim to objectivity has to be given up because one of the qualities of an objective description is that the properties of observers do not enter into it, do not influence and determine it. Heinz von Foerster's cryptically aphoristic definition of objectivity — another key statement of constructivism, and a topic of the first chapter in this book — can only be appreciated fully against this background: "Objectivity", he says, "is the subject's delusion that observing can be done without him."

Logical and rhetorical self-contradictions

We can, however, question the truth of this kind of truth and similar truths. Is it correct that everything depends on observers and that they are always present in their observations? What forces are at work in the real world of objects? When will objects resist the theses and theories we want to impress on them? How objective is the rejection of objective knowledge? Or more drastically: Is it true in an absolute sense that absolute truth is unknowable? Of course, questions of this kind cannot be answered, and certainly not in any definitive way; they are, as Heinz von Foerster would add, undecidable. We can only answer them personally for ourselves and we must, as a result, bear the burden of responsibility for such deeply personal acts of decision. Constructivist authors, who claim absolute truth for the assumption of the impossibility of attaining absolute truth, turn into meta-dogmatists and become entangled in a logical self-contradiction that may be expressed by the formula, "If they are right, they are wrong (and vice versa)." The use of an impersonal kind of language (exhibiting seemingly observer-unspecific characteristics) may, for this very reason, display a fundamental problem. A conventional researcher whose linguistic style excludes stories, parables, creative metaphors, and the description of personal thinking experiences, and who, in particular, clearly banishes all personal expressions from texts, must appear to write in a mode strongly suggesting claims to objectivity. Such language from constructivists and other sceptics creates a paradox, which we might term a *rhetorical self-contradiction*. In the case of a logical self-contradiction, statements are logically incompatible. The concept of a rhetorical self-contradiction means, however, that the chosen manner of expression, the diction, does not match the meaning to be conveyed. It indicates authority together with a claim to finality and ultimate certainty, which can in no way be justified if the self-chosen premises are adhered to. It insinuates, through stylistic choices, the possibility of ultimate justification and objective description — and simultaneously questions it, on the content level, by using a diction and a jargon of irrevocability that is incompatible with the fundamental beliefs presupposed, beliefs that ought to inspire a different, more open and, in particular, an observer-bound manner of presentation and discourse. We could also put it this way: writing about constructivism inevitably raises the question of form, which in itself involves tackling the problem of form.

Although the interviews presented in this book may strike readers as not equally successful, I still believe that conversation and dialogue are particularly well suited to present the constructivist theory of the observer. Dialogue partners may contradict each other and even quarrel; specific insights, which might appear to command universal validity, if formulated by a single author, may be playfully approached from different angles without pushing towards final harmony and a synthesis obscuring all contradictions. The process of the emergence and the fabrication of thoughts becomes the actual point of fixation of what is to be achieved. The results surfacing in a real conversation are junctures for constantly extending and alternating one's thoughts. The exaggerations and fixations, the disparities and provocations, appear to be instances of transition and elements of a progression that fails to end in a new absolute. They are means and instruments, not result and certainty. The posture of an all-encompassing and unbroken presentation, which is required by ultimate truths and monolithic edifices of thought, is thus disrupted. The form is the message; a conversation, if at all successful, is always an expression of the basic constructivist thesis that *reality as such* does not exist but that there is a multiverse of diverse interpretations. As soon as one has understood that reality is something ineluctably individual and necessarily manifold, one quickly realises that the persons asserting this view are not at all in favour of being congregated in a party of believing constructivists. The very designation *constructivism* in the book's title implies, as several interviewees emphasised, a consonance of thought that simply does not exist. There is a certain danger that the peculiar characteristics of individual research programmes and queries are lost under a label resembling a trendy slogan.

This is perhaps the reason why Humberto R. Maturana never uses the term in our conversation, why Heinz von Foerster prefers to be called a *curiosologist*, and why Helm Stierlin regards the era of constructivist textbooks with scepticism. It is a symptom, he says, of the coming to an end of a phase of creative anarchy, of wild, untethered thought production. There is the threat of an epistemological *biedermeier*. The constructivist thinking game is being turned into a norm, a new creed — a new truth. To avoid the fossilisation and dogmatisation of thinking, all so-called constructivists must constantly make clear that there can be no final proof and no observer-independent justification for their theses. Biology and brain research cannot, in any way, claim to be the trailblazers for the verification of constructivist assumptions; they can make them plausible, they can illustrate them, they can supply relevant indications, but they cannot prove their truth in an emphatic sense. Constructivism is itself only a construction (among many others); it cannot be tested for its truth but only for its utility, its viability. The main thing is, Ernst von Glasersfeld maintains in conversation, to develop effective procedures and assumptions, which will serve the purposes of particular observers. One must struggle to move forward, to explore whether one's theses and theories prove productive or whether the big unknown, ordinarily and quite roughly called *reality*, resists our interpretations. There are no plans for a new quest to conquer finality by way of seeking ultimate salvation in a modern variety of scepticism. On the contrary: "Any scepticism that is consistent can only be free-floating, well-founded but without foundations, or unfounded but with solid foundations, otherwise it will lose its magic and degenerate into dogmatism." (Fischer 1993, p. 96: translated from the German)

Bernhard Poerksen
Hamburg, February 2001

References

Fischer, H. R. (1993): Information, Kommunikation und Sprache. Fragen eines Beobachters. In H. R. Fischer (ed.), *Autopoiesis. Eine Theorie im Brennpunkt der Kritik*. Heidelberg Carl-Auer-Systeme, 67-97.

Maturana, H. R. (1979): Biology of Cognition. In H. R. Maturana/F. J. Varela, *Autopoiesis and Cognition. The Realization of the Living*. Boston: D. Reidel, 1-58.

Varela, F. (1975): A calculus for self-reference. *International Journal of General Systems* 2, 5-24.

CHAPTER 1

At each and every moment, I can decide who I am

Heinz von Foerster on the observer, dialogic life, and a constructivist philosophy of distinctions

© Thomas Reinagl, Wien

Heinz von Foerster (1911-2002) is held to be the "Socrates of cybernetics". Having studied physics in Vienna, he worked in various research laboratories in Germany and Austria, and after World War II also briefly as a journalist and as a consultant to a telephone company. At the same time, he wrote his first book, *Memory: A quantum-mechanical investigation* (published in Vienna, 1948). His theory of memory caught the attention of the founding figures of American cybernetics. They invited him; he immigrated to the USA in 1949. There, he was received into a circle of scientists that began to meet in the early fifties under the auspices of the Macy Foundation. He was made editor of the annual conference proceedings. The mathematician Norbert Wiener, whose book *Cybernetics* had just been published, John von Neumann, the inventor of the computer, the anthropologists Gregory Bateson and Margaret Mead, the neuropsychiatrist Warren S. McCulloch, together with more than a dozen other intellectual enthusiasts, formed the group essentially contributing to the so-called Macy Conferences.

In 1957, Heinz von Foerster was meanwhile appointed professor, founded the Biological Computer Laboratory (BCL) at the University of Illinois, which he directed until his retirement in 1976. At this institution, he brought together avant-garde artists and original minds from all over the world. In the inspiring climate of the BCL, philosophers and electrical engineers, biologists (e.g. Humberto R. Maturana and Francisco J. Varela), anthropologists and mathematicians, artists and logicians debated epistemological questions from inter-disciplinary perspectives deriving from both the sciences and the arts.

They dealt with the rules of computation in humans and machines and analysed the logical and methodological problems involved in the understanding of understanding and the observation of the observer. It is von Foerster's outstanding achievement to have brought into focus the inescapable prejudices and blind spots of the human observer approaching his apparently independent object of inquiry. His ethical stance demands constant awareness of one's blind spots, to accept, in a serious way, that one's apparently final pronouncements are one's own productions, and to cast doubt on certainties of all kinds and forms, while at the same time continually searching for other and new possibilities of thought.

The myth of objectivity

Poerksen: Every theory, every attitude, or worldview, rests on its own aphorisms and key statements that, if one probes their depths and thinks them through, encompass what is essential. Psychoanalysts follow Freud's thesis that humans are "not masters in their own house" because the subconscious reigns supreme there. The central formula of Marxism is: "Being determines consciousness." ("Das Sein bestimmt das Bewusstsein.") The behaviourist Skinner upholds the determinist thesis "Human behaviour is the function of variables in the environment." One of the key aphorisms of constructivism and your own world of ideas, it seems to me, may possibly be located in the writings of your friend, the biologist Humberto Maturana: "Anything said is said by an observer."

Von Foerster: The entree you have chosen seems very interesting to me — for there is always the question: With what claims and assumptions should we approach an area of thought? Where, how and when should we begin with the telling of a story? Moreover, what will happen afterwards? Will people pound their fists on the table and declare everything nonsense, or will they smile at you full of excitement? Considering Maturana's theorem in isolation and without all its implicit consequences will certainly not earn you special admiration. Nobody will exclaim: "Wow! What a revelation!" You might rather hear: "My God, if this is the fundamental tenet of his philosophy, then I prefer to go to the cinema or have a drink." This theorem, without its proper context, may appear ridiculous, annoying, or downright stupid.

Poerksen: What are some of the epistemological consequences — to formulate the question quite generally — if we take the statement seriously and try to build a system of thought upon it?

Von Foerster: One of the conclusions is that what a human being comprehends can no longer be externalised and be seen simply as given. The statement undermines our craving for objectivity and truth for we must not forget that it is a distinguishing feature of objective and true descriptions that the personal properties of the observer do not enter into them, do not influence or determine them in any way. They must not, it is claimed, be distorted or disturbed by an observer's predilections, personal idiosyncrasies, political or philosophical inclinations, or any other kind of club affiliation. I would say, however, that this whole concept is sheer madness, absolutely impossible. How can one demand a thing like that — and still remain a professor?! The moment you try to eliminate the properties of the observer, you create a vacuum: There isn't anyone left to observe anything — and to tell us about it.

Poerksen: The observer is the component that cannot be eliminated from a process of knowing.

Von Foerster: Exactly. There must always be someone who smells, tastes, hears, and sees. I have never really been able to understand, what the proponents of objective descriptions want to observe at all if they ban the human observer's personal view of things right from the start.

Poerksen: "Objectivity is a subject´s delusion," the *American Society for Cybernetics* quotes you, "that observing can be done without him."

Von Foerster: How can we get round the question: What can observers perceive who, according to the common definition of objectivity, are in fact blind, deaf and dumb, and who are not allowed to use their own language? What can they tell us? How are they to talk? Only an observer can observe. Without an observer, there is nothing.

Poerksen: If we, as you suggest, tie knowing inseparably to the knower, what sense and what function remains for the key concepts of realism, e.g. *reality*, *fact,* and *object*?

Von Foerster: If used at all, they will only serve as crutches, metaphors, and shortcuts. They may be used to state things and establish relations, without delving more profoundly into the questions involved. They will facilitate quick reference to specific points of relevance — a place, an object, a property — which are supposed to exist in the world, and to formulate corresponding statements. The danger lies in it being all too easy to forget that we are using crutches and metaphors and to believe that the world is *really* and *truthfully* represented by our descriptions. And that is the moment in which conflicts and hostilities and wars arise about the question what the facts are and who is in possession of the truth.

Poerksen: To take the knower — the observer — seriously also entails supplementing or even replacing ontological questions concerning the *What* — the object of knowing — by epistemological questions relating to the *How* — the process of knowing. What insights or perhaps what experiences have induced you personally to focus on the observer in your research and in your reflections? Was there an intellectual key experience?

Insights of a magician

Von Foerster: The experience occurred a very long time ago. At twelve or thirteen years of age, my cousin Martin and I — we grew up together like two inseparable brothers — began to practise magic. We invented our own acts, stunned the amazed grown-ups with our enthusiasm, and realised after a while that magic had nothing to do with mechanical things, false bottoms, tricks, optical illusions etc., which everybody is familiar with; the decisive thing was to create an atmosphere in which something unbelievable, something unexpected could happen, something nobody had ever seen. It is the spectator who invents a world in which girls are sawn apart and elephants float through the air. What instilled an awareness of the observer into me was the question: How can I create an atmosphere for a group of people, in which miracles may be seen? What sort of story must I tell, *how* must I tell it in order to make people accept it and make them work the miracles of the floating elephant and the sawn girl in their own individual ways? As a child or a youngster you simply perform your magic acts, you listen in amazement to what the grown-ups tell you about what they have seen, and perhaps you wonder what goes on in their brains. And this is what you later — when you are fifty, perhaps — describe as the *observer problem.*

Poerksen: Magicians are, if I am not mistaken, practising constructivists; they create visions and construct realities, which contradict the laws of gravity as well as the rules of probability and everyday life.

Von Foerster: This is the point. Magic, for me, was the original experience of constructivism: together with the other participants you invent a world in which elephants disappear and girls are sawn apart — and suddenly re-appear totally unharmed. What amused me and my cousin most was that the spectators who had apparently all seen the same event — the magic trick — often related quite different variations in the interval or after the show, which had nothing or very little to do with what we or other magicians had done. Mr Miller, Mr Jones, and Ms Cathy obviously created their own personal events. They saw girls sawn apart that were not, of course, sawn apart at all, neither had the elephants been made to vanish. These experiences drew my attention to the psychology of observing and the creation of a world: What happens, I asked myself, in the process of observing? Is that observer sitting in Hermann von Helmholtz's famous *locus observandi* and describing the world in a state of complete neutrality?

Poerksen: What do you think? What is the observer doing? What is going on?

Von Foerster: The customary view is: the observer sees the world, perceives it, and says what it is like. Observers supposedly occupy that strange *locus observandi* and watch — unconstrained by personality, individual taste, and idiosyncratic features — an independent reality. In contrast, I maintain that observers in action primarily look *into* themselves. What they are describing is *their* view of how the world appears to *them*. And good magicians are able to sense what kinds of world other persons would like to be real, at a certain moment, and they can help them to create these worlds successfully.

Poerksen: The magician's act, technically speaking, involves three components: the magician, the event, and the spectators. If we asked a solipsist, a realist, and a constructivist to describe what was happening, we would get quite different accounts. The solipsists would tell us that nothing of what they describe is real, but that everything is a chimera of our minds merely imagining the magician as well as a world that does not, in fact, exist. The realists would insist that observing is nothing but the mapping of reality onto the screen of our mind — and that the observers, the spectators, are deceived by the magician's trickery: they fall victim to an illusion that does not adequately represent the reality of what is independently existent. Your kind of constructivism occupies the middle ground between realism and solipsism: There is something there, you would probably say, something is really going on, and that seems beyond doubt; but it is just as certain that all human beings describe the reality of those events in their own ways and construct their very own worlds.

Von Foerster: I have an uncanny feeling that the language we are using at this moment in our conversation is playing tricks on us and producing all sorts of strange bubbles. You know what I want to talk about, and I know more or less, what I want to say. Still, I am not sure whether this kind of epistemological classification and this manner of linguistic embedding would enable other persons to grasp what you and I are getting at. This means: we must, for a moment, consider the language we use to express what we mean. The mere sentence "There is something there" seems to me to be poisoned by the presuppositions of realism. I am worried that the position you assign to me is holding some backdoor open through which that terrible notion of ontology may still gain entrance. Accepting this position, one may continue to speak of the existence of an external reality. And referring to an external reality and existence is a wonderful way of eliminating one's responsibility for what one is saying. That is the deep horror of ontology. You introduce the apparently innocent expression "there is..." which I once jokingly and somewhat pompously termed the *existential operator* and say with authoritarian violence: "It is so... there is..." But *why* is *what* there? And *who* asserts that something is the case?

Poerksen: The fact that you reject any prefabricated terminology and show a noticeable aversion towards any clean and, as it were, unadulterated epistemological classification of your ideas, seems to me to be an important indication of a fundamental problem: How can we speak about the act of observing, the observer, and the observed, in a way that does justice to the dynamic processes involved?

Von Foerster: This is an incredibly difficult problem because we are working with a medium — language. Being tied to that medium, we are seduced to speak in a way that suggests the existence of a world independent from us. One of my great desires is to learn to control my language in such a way as to keep my ethics implicit, whether I am dealing with politics, science, or poetry, so that it is always evident that I myself am the point of reference of the observations I am offering. I would like to invent a language or form of communication — and perhaps it will have to be poetry, music, or dance — that would release something in another person, so that any reference to an external world or reality, to any "there is..." would be superfluous; any such reference, so I imagine, would no longer be needed. To do this successfully, however, one must be firmly anchored in that world. Moreover, one problem always remains: What other form can we invent that would also deal with the problem of form?

Poerksen: In my view, the actual question is: How can we speak or write in such a way as to make the observer-dependence of all knowledge visible whenever we speak or write? How can we show that our descriptions of the world are not the descriptions of an external reality but the descriptions of an observer who *believes* they are descriptions of an external reality?

Von Foerster: The problem is a dialogue between you and me that does not rely on any reference to something external. When I insist, for instance, that it is *you* producing this view of things, that it is not something out there, not the so-called objective reality, that we can fall back on, then a strange fore-grounding of you, the person speaking, is effected. General-ised expressions beginning with "There is..." are replaced by expressions beginning with "I think that..." We use, to say it somewhat pompously again, the *self-referential operator* "I think..." and abandon the existential operator "there is." In this way, a completely different relation emerges that paves the way for a free dialogue.

Poerksen: If you do not want to talk about subject, object, and the process of knowing — the observer, the observed, and the process of observing — on the basis of a form of language established in the academic world involving classic epistemological concepts, what ways of talking can we turn to?

Separation or connection

Von Foerster: I cannot offer a general solution but I would like to present a short dramatic scene that I once wrote because it might help to escape the grip of predetermined forms. The scene is performed for an audience in a baroque theatre. The lights are dimmed, the impressive red velvet curtain rises, and the stage comes into full view. There is a tree, a man, and a woman, all forming a triangle. The man points at the tree and says: "There is a tree." — The woman says: "How do you know that there is a tree?" — The man: "Because I see it!" — With a brief smile, the woman says: "Aha!" — The curtain comes down. — I contend, this drama has been discussed, mis-understood, and even attacked for thousands of years, a drama that is well suited to illuminate the debates of questions of knowledge and the role of an external world. Whom do we want to trust, whom do we want to refer to? The man? The woman? Since primeval times, the undecidable question has been haunting us whether to side with the man or with the woman. The man affirms the observer-independent existence of the tree and the environment, the woman draws his atten-tion to the fact that he only knows of the tree because *he* sees it, and that seeing is, therefore, primary. We must now ask our-selves which of these attitudes we are prepared to accept. The man relies on his external reference, the woman points out to him that the perception of the tree is tied to *his* observation. However, this little piece does not only deal, as might be suspected, with objectivity and subjectivity or different epistemological positions. Something else is much more important: The man separates himself from the world, the woman connects herself with what she describes.

Poerksen: This is, then, another contrast that comes into play here. It is not primarily concerned with the distinction between subjectivity and objectivity but with the question as to whether I connect myself to the world, or whether my epistemological position forces me to see myself as distinct from it, as a person observing it from an imaginary *locus observandi.*

Von Foerster: This is a good way of putting it. The man in my little drama looks at the passing and unfolding universe as if through a keyhole, at the trees, the things, and the other people. He does not have to feel responsible, he represents a sort of keyhole or peephole philosophy, he is a *voyeur.* Nothing concerns him because nothing touches him. Indifference becomes excusable. The woman insists that it is only a human being can see and observe. The attitude of the detached describers is opposed to the attitude of the compassionate participants who consider themselves as part of the world. Each one acts on the basis of the premise: Whatever I do, will change the world! I am the world, and the world is me!

Poerksen: What are the consequences of this experience or knowledge of connectedness?

Von Foerster: What we call the world is, all of a sudden, no longer something hostile but appears to be an organ, an inseparable part of one's own body. The universe and the self have become united. We have to shoulder responsibility for our actions; we can no longer retire to the position of the passive recorder who describes a static and supposedly timeless existence. We have been made aware that every action — even the mere lifting of an arm — may create a new universe that did not exist before. Knowing this — or better, sensing it and feeling it — excludes any kind of static vision; on the contrary, everything is now in constant flux, every situation is new, nothing is eternal, nothing can ever be as it once used to be.

Poerksen: I am quite in favour of this description of an observer-dependent universe. Nevertheless, objections immediately come to mind. We perceive the world as something that has developed and grown, and the experience of the stability of our human condition is definitely quite comforting. Its regularities seem reliable, they provide orientation, allow us to make plans and to face the future with certain expectations. What I want to say is: The attitude you describe contradicts our everyday experience and it is, in addition, psychologically unattractive.

Von Foerster (laughing): Absolutely right. I completely agree with you.

Poerksen: You agree with me? Do you not want to convince me of the correctness of an observer-dependent state of the world?

Von Foerster: For God's sake! I would not dream of trying to convince you because that would cause your view to vanish. It would then be lost. All I can attempt is to act the magician so that you may be put in a position to convince yourself. Perhaps I might succeed in inviting you to re-interpret, for a moment, the security you find so attractive as something undermining openness. For even security and stability of circumstances may get persons into great trouble at certain stages in their lives, when they, for instance, do not realise that the circumstances constraining them might be completely different ones, and that it is in their power to change them.

Poerksen: As you are unwilling to convince me, what is, then, for you, the purpose of a dispute or a conversation?

Von Foerster: I would like to answer with a little story about the world of Taoism, which has fascinated me since childhood. My uncle, Erwin Lang, was taken prisoner by the Russian forces soon after the outbreak of World War I and deported to Siberia. When the Russian Empire collapsed in 1917, he managed to escape to China. He finally reached the German settlement Tsingtau where he met the scholar Richard Wilhelm, the translator of the *I Ching,* who introduced him to the ideas of Taoism. Through his help and recommendation, Erwin Lang was accepted by a Taoist monastery at which he arrived after a two days walk. Still uncertain whether the War was over and the fighting had stopped, he asked one of the monks for newspapers. Of course, the monk said, we have newspapers; we have, in fact, an enormous library. My uncle was impressed and asked for a copy of the Austrian *Neue Freie Presse*. Certainly, the monk said, we have newspapers from all over the world. He took him to the archive in the monastery and, after a short search, produced the most recent issue of the *Neue Freie Presse* available. It was the issue of 15 February 1895. Of course, Erwin Lang was somewhat consternated and pointed out to the monk that the paper was more than 20 years old. The monk looked at him and said: "So what?! What are 20 years?" At that moment, my uncle began to understand Taoism: Time did not play any role in this world; topical news value was of no importance.

Poerksen: You are unwilling to convince me, and you refuse to discredit other, or antagonist, positions, but you use history and stories — your little parable seems a case in point — in order to make further possibilities of perceiving accessible.

Von Foerster: This interpretation is most welcome. My goal is indeed to present different perspectives that may, or may not, be taken up. To return to the beginning of our conversation: Whether we accept the theorem of my friend, Humberto Maturana ("Anything said is said by an observer"), and whether we consider ourselves connected with the world or separate from it, — we are confronted by undecidable questions. Decidable questions are, in a certain sense, already decided through their given framework; their decidability is secured by specific rules and formalisms — for example, syllogisms, syntax, or arithmetic — that must be accepted. The question, for instance, whether the number 7856 is divisible by two, is easy to answer because we know that numbers with an even final number are divisible by two. Paul Feyerabend's notorious slogan, *anything goes,* does not apply here because the rules of arithmetic force us to proceed in a certain way in order to find an answer. Undecidable questions, on the contrary, are unsolvable in principle; they can never really be clarified. Nobody knows, I would claim, whether the man or the woman in my little drama is right, and whether it is more correct to consider oneself connected with the world or separate from it. This situation of fundamental undecidability is an invitation to decide for oneself. For this decision, however, one must shoulder the responsibility oneself.

Monologic and dialogic

Poerksen: Reviewing our conversation about the observer, I cannot help noticing that you keep returning to the interaction of human beings. To put it differently, as a kind of thesis: For you, observers are not isolated figures; they always exist in a field of relations, in a community. Your own ideas, too, always appear embedded in actual relationships, in personal experiences and personal thoughts.

Von Foerster: The observer as a strange singularity in the universe does not attract me, indeed; you are quite right there. This kind of concept will probably be of interest to a neurophysiologist or neuroanatomist, whereas I am fascinated by images of duality, by binary metaphors like dance and dialogue where only a duality creates a unity. Therefore, the statement that opened our conversation — "Anything said is said by an observer" — is floating freely, in a sense. It exists in a vacuum as long as it is not embedded in a social structure because speaking is meaningless, and dialogue is impossible, if no one is listening. So I have added a corollary to that theorem, which I named with all due modesty *Heinz von Foerster's Corollary Nr. 1*: "Everything said is said *to* an observer." Language is not monologic but always dialogic. Whenever I say or describe something, I am after all not doing it for myself but to make someone else know and understand what I am thinking or intending to do.

Poerksen: What happens when other observers are involved?

Von Foerster: We get a triad consisting of the observers, the languages, and the relations constituting a social unit. The addition produces the nucleus and the core structure of society, which consists of two people using language. Due to the recursive nature of their interactions, stabilities arise; they generate observers and their worlds, who recursively create other stable worlds through interacting in language. Therefore, we can call a funny experience *apple* because other people also call it *apple*. Nobody knows, however, whether the green colour of the apple you perceive, is the same experience as the one I am referring to with the word *green*. In other words, observers, languages, and societies are constituted through recursive linguistic interaction, although it is impossible to say which of these components came first and which were last —

remember the comparable case of hen, egg, and cock — we need all three in order to have all three.

Poerksen: I do not want to over-interpret this transformation of a monologic idea, which is tied to a single observer, into a dialogic concept involving two or more observers in interaction, but it seems to me to contain some hidden anthropology; not a hierarchic one, to be sure, which would compare human beings with machines, animals, or gods, but an anthropology of relations, of interdependence, of You and I. When you relate one human being to another, you are reflecting on the essence of humanity and its potential: there is one human being and there is another — this seems to me to be your point of reference.

Von Foerster: Very well put, indeed. A human being is a human being together with another human being; that is what a human being is. I exist through another I, I see myself through the eyes of the Other, and I shall not tolerate that this relationship is destroyed by the idea of the objective knowledge of an independent reality, which tears us apart and makes the Other an object which is distinct from me. This world of ideas has nothing to do with proof, it is a world one must experience, see, or simply be. When one suddenly experiences this sort of communality, one begins to dance together, one senses the next common step and one's movements fuse with those of the other into one and the same person, into a being that can see with four eyes. Reality becomes communality and community. When the partners are in harmony, twoness flows like oneness, and the distinction between leading and being led has become meaningless. In my view, the best description of this sort of communality is by Martin Buber. He is a very important philosopher for me.

Poerksen: Buber is not just the protagonist of a dialogic philosophy but also a religious scholar and writer, and a mystic. For him, the dialogue between an I and a You mirrors the eternal dialogue with God.

Von Foerster: I feel deep respect for his religious beliefs and feelings but I am unable to share them, really, and perhaps would not like to, anyway. Should his religious orientation be the source of his incredible strength and depth, I can only admire him the more.

Poerksen: What were the seminal experiences that oriented you towards a dialogic life?

Von Foerster: Among the most important is an encounter with the Viennese psychiatrist and pastoral curer of souls, Viktor Frankl. He had survived the concentration camp but had lost his wife and his parents, and he practised again in the psychiatric institution in Vienna from where he had been deported years before. A married couple had also miraculously survived the Nazi terror, each partner in a different camp. Husband and wife had returned to Vienna, had found each other, had naturally been overjoyed to find the partner alive, and had begun a new life together. About a month after their reunion, the wife died of a disease she had contracted in the camp. The husband was absolutely shattered and desperate; he stopped eating and just sat on a stool in his kitchen. Finally, friends managed to persuade him to go and see Viktor Frankl whose special authority as a camp survivor was beyond doubt. Both men talked for more than an hour — then Frankl abruptly changed the topic and said: "Suppose, God gave me the power to create a woman completely identical with your wife. She would crack the same jokes, use the same language and the same gestures, — in brief, you would be unable to spot any difference. Do you want me to ask for God's help in order to create such a woman?" — The man shook his head, stood up, thanked Frankl, left his practice, and started up his life again. When I heard about this story, I went to see Frankl immediately — we were working together professionally on a radio programme broadcast every Friday, at the time -, and I asked him: "Viktor, how was that possible? What did you do?" — "Heinz, it is very simple," Frankl said, "we see ourselves through the eyes of the other. When she died, he was blind. But when he realised that he was blind, he was able to see again."

In the beginning was the distinction

Poerksen: Perhaps we could now, with a modest topical jump, leave all types of observers behind, and deal with the process of observing itself. Every observation, George Spencer-Brown writes in his famous treatise *Laws of Form*, begins with an act of distinction. More precisely: observations operate with two-valued distinctions one of which may be designated. Therefore, if I want to designate something, I have to decide about a distinction first. The choice of a distinction determines what I can see. Using the distinction between *good* and *bad* I can — wherever I am looking — observe other things than when I am using the distinctions between *rich* und *poor, beautiful* and *ugly, new* and *old* or *ill* and *healthy.* And so on. Consequently, observing means distinguishing and designating.

Von Foerster: Correct, yes. George Spencer-Brown formulates: "Draw a distinction and a universe comes into being." The act of distinction is taken to be the fundamental operation of cognition; it generates realities that are assumed to reside in an external space separated from the person of the distinguisher. A simple example: We draw a circle on a piece of paper; we create, in this way, two worlds, one *outside* and one *inside,* which may now be designated more precisely. In other words, if we follow George Spencer-Brown's argument, before something can be named or designated, before we can describe the space within the circle more exactly, the world has been divided into two parts: it now consists of what we have named, on the one hand, and what is obscured by the name, the rest of the world, on the other.

Poerksen: When you encountered these ideas — you wrote one of the first widely noted reviews of *Laws of Form* — what fascinated you, in particular?

Von Foerster: What fascinated me, at the time, and still fascinates me now, is that the formal apparatus, the logical machinery, which Spencer-Brown developed, enables us to solve the classical problem of the paradox that has troubled logicians ever since the days of Epimenides. Epimenides, a Cretan, said: "I am a Cretan. All Cretans lie." He might as well have said: "I am a liar!" What do you do with someone who says: "I am a liar"?! Do you believe him? If so, he cannot be lying, he must have told the truth. If he told the truth, however, he lied, because he said: "I am a liar." The ambivalence of this statement is that it is true when it is false, and that it is false when it is true. The speaker steps inside what is spoken, and all of a sudden, the function turns into an argument of itself. Such a statement is like a virus and may destroy an entire logical system, or a set of axioms, and cannot, of course, be acceptable to honest logicians following the Aristotelean creed: "A meaningful statement must be either true or false." In the twentieth century, Bertrand Russell and Albert North Whitehead attempted to resolve the liar-paradox by simply prohibiting, as it were, self-referential expressions of this kind. Their theory of types and their escape into a meta-language, however, did not seem satisfactory to me. I have always thought, although I did not know an elegant solution, that language itself ought to be the meta-language of the logicians. Language must be able to speak about itself; that is to say, the operator (language) must become the operand (language). We need a sort of *salto mortale*. George Spencer-Brown has developed an operator that is constructed in such a way as to permit application to itself. His operator can operate on itself and, in this way, becomes part of itself and the world it creates.

Poerksen: How can these ideas be related to epistemology, in particular, to the observer, the central figure of our conversation?

Von Foerster: Whenever I want to say something about myself — and I maintain that everything I am saying is said about myself — I must be aware that speaking involves a fundamental paradox that has to be dealt with. George Spencer-Brown's formalism bridges the customary division between seeing and seen. The epistemology we might envisage against this background is dynamic, not static. It has to do with becoming, not being. Spencer-Brown refuses to start out from the supposition that a statement can only *be* true or false; the formalism invented by him reveals the dynamics of states. As in a flip-flop mechanism, the truth of an expression generates its falsity, and its falsity generates its truth, and so on. He shows that the paradox generates a new dimension: time.

Poerksen: I think it would be worthwhile to describe the philosophy of distinctions that has developed since the publication of *Laws of Form* in detail. Let me, therefore, ask you: What will happen, for example, when I introduce the distinction between *good* and *evil* into the world and make it the foundation of my observations?

Von Foerster: The distinction between *good* and *evil* and the universe created in this way may be used to form sentences and to make statements. Now, it is possible to say of an elephant or of a company director that they are good or particularly wicked. We can build up a calculus of statements, cascades of expressions, which deal with human persons, animals, directors, or elephants. What tends to be overlooked usually is that these distinctions are not out there in the world, are not properties of things and objects but properties of our descriptions of the world. The objects there will forever remain a mystery but their descriptions reveal the properties of observers and speakers, whom we can get to know better in this way. The elephants have no idea of what we are doing, the elephants are simply elephants; *we* make them good or wicked elephants.

Poerksen: Is it correct to say, as you claim, that the intrinsic properties of objects and things in the world do *not* become effective in our descriptions?

Von Foerster: In my view, objects correspond to the sensorimotor experience of a human being who suddenly realises that it cannot simply move everywhere, that there is something blocking its movement, something *standing in the way*, some *ob-ject*. This limitation of behaviour generates objects. As soon as I have acquired enough practice and have experienced these objects often enough, some stability in the experience of limitation has developed and I am in a position to give a name to the item of my sensorimotor skill and competence, call the *ob-ject* a cup, or glasses, or Bernhard Poerksen. This is to say: What I designate as glasses or cup is, strictly speaking, a symbol for my nervous system's competence to generate stabilities, to compute invariants.

Poerksen: What sort of truth status would you claim for this thesis? Is it an ontologically correct theory of object formation; are objects *really* constituted in this way?

Von Foerster: Let me return the question: What do you think? What would you prefer, what would you like better?

Poerksen: Are you suggesting it is a matter of taste?

Von Foerster: If *you* want it this way, then it may also be a matter of taste. If you, however, prefer to live in a world where the properties of your descriptions are the properties of the world itself, then that is fine.

Poerksen: People will condemn this as absurd.

Von Foerster: Naturally, this is one of the usual reactions to someone thinking along different lines. The persons that come up with objections of this kind will have to live with the consequences. They create this world for themselves. I am only myself, I am rolling along, I can only try to communicate what I like, what I see, what I find fascinating, and what I want to distinguish. Whether other people consider me a scientist, a constructivist, a magician, a philosopher, a curiosologist, or simply a brat, that is their problem; and it is due to the distinctions they draw.

Blind to one's own blindness

Poerksen: For you, the individual — socially anchored, of course — is evidently the central reality-creating instance. The sociologist Niklas Luhmann, however, who refers explicitly both to Spencer-Brown and your work, only speaks of the operation of observ*ing*, — never the observ*er*. He wrote book after book on science, art, religion, politics, and economics, reconstructing the forms of observation and the central sets of distinctions at work in these social domains, to which everyone entering them must necessarily orientate.

Von Foerster: Le me just point out that society, too, is a relational structure; it is a framework according to which we may, but need not, think. In my work, however, the self and the individual are central and present from the start. The reason is that I can conceive of responsibility only as something personal, not as dependent on anything social. You cannot hold a society responsible for anything — you cannot shake its hand, ask it to justify its actions — and you cannot enter into a dialogue with it; whereas I can speak with another self, a you.

Poerksen: What you mean is, I think, that observers — human beings — can indeed decide what distinctions they want to make. My objection is that the world never is — in Spencer-Brown's terminology — an *unmarked space*, but that we are all pressured in many ways, and even condemned, to reproduce the distinctions and views of our own groups, of parents, friends, and institutions. To quote but a blatant example: the children growing up in a sectarian community will obviously absorb its reality.

Von Foerster: This is possible, no doubt. On the other hand, I remain convinced that these people, these individuals, can always opt out of such a network and escape from the sectarian system. They have this freedom, I would claim, but they are all too often completely unable to actually see it. They are blind to their own blindness and do not see that they do not see; they are incapable of realising that there are still possibilities for action. They have created their blind spot and are frozen in their everyday mechanisms and think there is no way out. The uncanny thing, actually, is that sects and dictators always manage to make actually existing freedom invisible for some time. All of a sudden, citizens become zombies or Nazis committing themselves to condemning freedom and responsibility by saying: "I was ordered to kill these people, I had no choice! I merely executed orders!" Even in such a situation, it is obviously possible to refuse. It would be a great decision, possibly leading to one's own death but still an act of incredible quality: "No, I will not do it. I will not kill anyone!" In brief, it is my view that freedom always exists. *At each and every moment, I can decide who I am.* Moreover, in order to render, and keep, this visible I have been pleading for a form of education and communality that does not restrict or impede the visibility of freedom and the multitude of opportunities but actively supports them. My ethical imperative is, therefore: "Act always so as to increase the number of choices."

Poerksen: But how can we re-invent ourselves at each and any moment? Surely, that is out of the question; the world — all the inescapable constraints on our lives — simply will not allow it. Here is my counter-thesis: In the act of observing, we reproduce either old orders or systems of distinctions, or we develop new ones from or against them. Therefore, the freedom and arbitrariness of constructions is massively reduced.

Von Foerster: It is certainly not my contention that the invention of realities is completely arbitrary and wilful and would allow me to see the sky blue at first, then green, and after opening my eyes again, not at all. Of course, every human being is tied into a social network, no individual is an isolated wonder phenomenon but dependent on others and must — to say it metaphorically — dance with others and construct reality through communality. The embedding into a social network necessarily leads to a reduction of arbitrariness through communality; however, it does not at all change the essentially given freedom. We make appointments, identify with others and invent common worlds — which one may give up again. The kinds of dance one chooses along this way may be infinitely variable.

Drop a distinction!

Poerksen: If I understand correctly, human beings are — together with others — capable of creating reality, in a positive sense. However, what are we to do about realities that we reject and do not want to create at all? Can we escape from them through negation?

Von Foerster: No, I do not think so. Ludwig Wittgenstein's *Tractatus-logico-philosophicus* made me see this clearly for the first time. There is the famous consideration that speaking about a proposition *"p"* and its negation *"non p"* means speaking of the same thing. The negation is in fact an affirmation. This is the mistake committed by my dear friends, the revolutionaries, who want to depose a king. They keep shouting loudly and clearly: "Down with the king!" That is, of course, free propaganda for the king who should, in fact, thank his enemies: "Thank you very much for mentioning me so frequently and for not stopping to call out my name!" If I negate a person, an idea, or an ideal, loudly and clearly, the final separation has not yet been achieved. The negated phenomenon will return and take centre stage again.

Poerksen: Who wants to get rid of something finally must neither describe it positively nor deny it, in order to achieve complete separation. What is to be done, then?

Von Foerster: Something different must be done. I suggest that certain distinctions are excluded because I have noticed in many discussions that their basis involves concepts that lead nowhere but only generate conflicts and hostilities. The negation of stupidity is no less stupid because it forces us to go on dealing with stupidity. To make these considerations clear I should like to speak, for a moment, about the *place-value logic* devised by the philosopher Gotthard Günther. In his papers, he analyses the emergence of a proposition, its logical place. Even talking about a king who is then either celebrated or shouted down by revolutionaries requires, according to

Günther, a certain place. However, this place may be refused in order to prevent any talk about kings. In this way, a new kind of logic arises. The simple dichotomy of affirmation and negation is left behind; certain propositions are marked with a *rejection-value* in order to make clear that they do not belong to the category of propositions under discussion.

Poerksen: Can you describe this kind of place — the basis that is required by every proposition as the condition of its possibility — more precisely?

Von Foerster: I think the Russians understood this idea very well. I once took part in a conference in Moscow in the era of Khrushchev who sought to bring about a new kind of interaction between bureaucrats and humankind. One day I took a stroll in one of the small parks near the Lenin mausoleum. I saw the statues of the Great Russian military leaders cut in stone and sitting on huge pedestals, staring into the void with their large moustaches. Suddenly I saw a pedestal without a statue, empty. Joseph Stalin cut in stone had once stood on it. In this way, the present government expressed its rejection of Stalin. Had the pedestal been removed as well — the place of the logical proposition in Gotthard Günther's theory — this kind of negation would not have been possible. They were very well aware of that!

Poerksen: This means that we can get rid of concepts simply by stopping to mention them, relegating them to a domain of non-existence, taking away their pedestal and their foundation, as it were. They drop back into an amorphous and shapeless sphere, which is cognitively inaccessible to us because it is not marked by distinctions and indications. In this case, George Spencer-Brown's fundamental imperative must be changed from *"Draw* a distinction!" to *"Drop* a distinction!"

Von Foerster: This is an excellent new operator: "Drop a distinction!" However, this sort of approach seems to have been known to journalists in Austria for some time; they say there that the best way of demolishing an idea or a person is to stop mentioning them. The formula is: "Do not even ignore!" If you want to destroy a politician and president of a country it is best not to write about his extramarital contacts with interns and other women; this would be wrong because the mere mentioning of his name makes people aware again of his existence and may make them say: What a handsome man! It is much more effective to speak about the weather and the weather frogs. And the politician immediately disappears.

Mysticism and metaphysics

Poerksen: Let me attempt a brief résumé. In the process of reality construction, we draw distinctions, we negate distinctions, reject them, try to distance ourselves from them, and sometimes drop them completely in order to get rid of unwanted concepts. We are left with the tricky question what might exist behind the universe that we have constructed. What exists beyond the space we have created through our distinctions? Can you offer an answer, perhaps a very personal one?

Von Foerster: Let me tell you a little story about a personal experience of mine. A few years ago, I was invited to a large conference and participated in a workshop called *Beyond Constructivism*, organised by a charming French lady scientist. People asked me, too, what was beyond constructivism. My answer was: "Ladies and gentlemen, last night, after I had heard of this workshop, I could not go to sleep for a long time because the question troubled me considerably. When I finally did catch some sleep, my grandmother appeared to me in a dream. Of course, I asked her instantly: "Grandmama, what is beyond constructivism?" — "Do not tell anyone, Heinz," she said, "I will let you in on the secret — constructivism!"

Poerksen: We can never go beyond our distinguishing and constructing of worlds.

Von Foerster: Exactly. The distinction creates the space. Without this basis, you cannot ask the question regarding the space and the world beyond the space.

Poerksen: Still, if we are to believe the reports of eastern mystics, there seem to be states of consciousness that are not constrained by the ordinary human forms of distinctions. Concluding your review of *Laws of Form,* you refer yourself to a "state of ultimate wisdom" and to the "core of a calculus of love in which all distinctions are suspended and all is one."

Von Foerster: That is indeed what I wrote; no more need be said because that is precisely what I wanted to say. I would be grateful if we could simply let that utterance be as it is and not take it to pieces as in an academic seminar.

Poerksen: It seems to me that you have developed a way of speaking that offers indications and hints at things you do not want to pursue any further once you have drawn attention to them.

Von Foerster: I am concerned with inviting people to look. If you are prepared to look, you may see, but you have to look first. This is what I want to make clear.

Poerksen: What do you want to show?

Von Foerster: That it is possible to show. Whatever someone sees is up to them.

Poerksen: I do not follow.

Von Foerster: I understand. However, in many cases, unanswerability and answerlessness generate insight.

Poerksen: What you call *answerlessness*, could just as well be the chiffre of a mystic: in this space of uncertainty we might again be able to envisage something absolute and "totally different ".

Von Foerster: The very attempt to understand something completely ordinary immediately confronts us with puzzles and wonders that we usually pass by and leave unnoticed in our everyday lives. Most of these cannot be explained in any serious sense; in my view, we will never be able to penetrate them and remove or even destroy their awesome quality. The knowledge we have of our world is to me like the tip of an iceberg; it is like the tiny bit of ice sticking out of the water, whereas our ignorance reaches far down into the deepest depths of the ocean. Such a claim of principled inexplicability and awesomeness undoubtedly makes me a mystic. I would be a metaphysician if I claimed to have an answer to this inexplicability.

CHAPTER 2

We can never know what goes on in somebody else's head

Ernst von Glasersfeld on truth and viability,
language and knowledge, and the premises of
constructivist education

Ernst von Glasersfeld (b. 1917) studied mathematics in Zürich and Vienna, was a farmer in County Dublin during the War, and worked as a journalist in Italy from 1947. There he met the philosopher and cybernetician Silvio Ceccato who, in the beginning stages of the computer age, had gathered a team of researchers in order to carry out projects of computational linguistic analysis and automatic language translation. Von Glasersfeld became a close collaborator of Ceccato's, translated for him, and developed projects of his own. In 1966, he moved to the USA where he was made a professor of cognitive psychology at the University of Georgia in 1970. Three principal research interests have made him one of the well-known founders of constructivism. He systematically scoured the history of European philosophy for varieties of epistemological scepticism and set up an ancestral gallery reaching back to the insights of the ancient sceptics of the 4th century B.C. He replaced the classical realist concept of truth by the idea of viability: theories need not and do not correspond with what is real, he says, but they must be practicable and useful, they must be viable. Finally, he introduced the work of the Swiss developmental psychologist, Jean Piaget, into the constructivist debate.

Jean Piaget, in his book *La construction du réel chez l'enfant*, constructs a model of how knowledge is created and developed through the confirmation or disappointment of expectations (or more precisely: of particular patterns of action, so-called schemes). A model of this kind has profound consequences for the conception of learning and teaching: it eliminates the reification of information and knowledge, the conception of knowledge as a substance that can be transferred from the teacher's head to the empty heads of students. The mechanical idea of teaching evaporates. We must face the ineluctable subjectivity of meanings and given cognitive patterns. From this perspective, the acquisition of knowledge no longer appears to be a passive reception of information but a creative activity. The upshot is that teaching someone something will only be successful if it is oriented towards the reality of that someone.

Ernst von Glasersfeld is, at present, with the Scientific Reasoning Research Institute of the University of Massachusetts. There he works on models of teaching and learning that apply the theory of constructivism to school practice.

The God's eye view

Poerksen: According to the famous definition by Thomas Aquinas, truth is *adaequatio intellectus et rei*, the correspondence between mind and object. Idea and world agree, it is assumed, they enter into exact correspondence. The object and the predication about the object have the same structure, as it were. The school of thought of constructivism, whose prominent representative you are, challenges this correspondence-based conception of truth and insists that knowledge of truth according to this understanding is impossible.

Von Glasersfeld: I am certainly not the first nor the only one to take this view; the pre-Socratic philosophers already formulate it — just remember Xenophanes, the sophists, and the school of Pyrrhon. They were fully aware that the ideas human beings formed on the basis of their experiences could never mirror a reality independent from them. Xenophanes states that it can never be established whether some image of reality is completely correct because it is impossible to verify its correctness even if it were the case. We can never step outside our perceptual and conceptual functions; all our examinations and tests concerning the relation between image and reality as such are, in any case, inevitably shaped by our instruments of experience.

Poerksen: To grasp the truth, one would have to leave our bodies, if I follow your thinking, in order to observe the absolute from a completely neutral point of view.

Von Glasersfeld: Exactly. Some recent philosophers have called this view from outside "the God´s eye view." The problem is now, however, that even God — if we want to regard Him/Her as a rational Being — is confronted by the very same problem: He/She needs an apparatus for experience — and that means that even God's experiences would be dependent on that apparatus. I do not believe, however, that we can comprehend God. The God's Eye View is a metaphor for the impossibility of attaining an uncorrupted image of reality as such.

Poerksen: This consideration appears to me somewhat anthropomorphist, to put it mildly. You are presenting God's view as if it were — like our human view — conditioned and preformed by a priori categories and forms of perception.

Von Glasersfeld: If I decide to remain within the bounds of rationality, I can only use human reason, and human rational thinking is always anthropomorphic. I could, of course, argue like a mystic, as an apophatic theologian, who says: if God possesses all the ascribed qualities, if God is omniscient, ubiquitous, eternal, then God is obviously totally different from the world that we human beings experience. And as we abstract all our concepts from our world of experience we will never be able to comprehend God by means of our concepts. This view seems central to me for two reasons. Firstly, the mystics arguing in this way formulate the perfectly logical assumption that something that is believed to exist outside their world of experience can never be grasped in terms derived from that world of experience. Secondly, they explicitly separate rational knowledge from mystical knowledge; both these forms of knowledge may exist side by side but they are fundamentally incompatible. This is most important for me.

Poerksen: Is it not rather striking that we, in this conversation about the possibility of comprehending the absolute, immediately come to talk about God? My impression is that the way you speak about the absolute resembles the way certain mystics describe God as the Inconceivable and as the "entirely other" Being.

Von Glasersfeld: Perfectly right. Scientific and religious ways of speaking also resemble each other in that they often purport to offer absolute knowledge. I find that parallel also quite amusing at times. The belief of some scientists to propagate the truth can easily be revealed a delusion because in the history of science nothing ever stays the same; theories and models of reality constantly change.

Poerksen: However, you too, as long as you remain faithful to your premises, cannot know with complete certainty whether any one of these theories corresponds with absolute reality or not. The unconditional negation of a correspondence between world and idea would obviously be a sort of *negative ontology*, a further variety of absolutism.

Von Glasersfeld: It is quite conceivable, of course, that one of our constructions, by coincidence, turns out to be a perfect match; but even such a theoretical and, in my eyes, rather improbable possibility would still not be sufficient to justify and determine that we have been successful — that our assumptions correspond with absolute reality. If we assert that our conceptions correspond with the world, then we are, I believe, obliged to prove this correspondence. And if we fail to do so, then correspondence-based assertions merely have the status of unwarranted theses.

Poerksen: It seems to me that your criterion of truth is that we cease to exist as persons when we observe and that the knowledge we manage to acquire is strictly independent from the cognitive instruments we use. You demand something impossible, and therefore you are immune to any kind of criticism.

Von Glasersfeld: I do not feel insecure with my views at all, and I know that I am in very good company; as already mentioned, the sceptics have, since the time of the Pre-Socratics, repeatedly pointed out that we can never compare our image of reality with reality as such, but that we can only compare images with images. Innumerable philosophers have racked their brains in order to refute this claim; not a single one has succeeded in providing proof for the correspondence between world and idea. For this reason, they have turned to metaphysics, i.e. into mysticism.

The fault of evolutionary epistemology

Poerksen: May I start another attempt, and from a different perspective, to justify the belief that there must be some systematic connection between our perceptions and the real world? Surely, we could argue that the perceptual apparatus of humans has adapted to given realities through constant and sometimes fatal trials and errors during the course of evolution. This was the view of the ethologist and evolutionary epistemologist Konrad Lorenz, who thought that the course of evolution effected a gradual approximation of the Kantian *thing-in-itself,* the real world. Constructions that fail to match reality would simply be destroyed by the mechanism of natural selection.

Von Glasersfeld: As I see it, we must always keep in mind that the theory of evolution and all the perspectives that appear to follow from it necessarily, are only models that we have constructed and that may be replaced by other models tomorrow. This is Konrad Lorenz's mistake, I think: he sees the theory of evolution as an ontological description, assuming that animals and humans have *factually* and *in reality* evolved in a certain way. Now this is an empirically well-founded hypothesis but empirical assumptions can never support ontology. We can certainly say that we have invented the categories of space and time because they are particularly useful and fit the reality of our experience. However, good functioning can never be proof of mirroring the external world. This is why I prefer to speak of *viability* in order to stress that we must always reckon with other possibilities of compatibility.

Poerksen: Konrad Lorenz formulates: "The adaptation to specific environmental conditions is equivalent to the acquisition of information about these environmental conditions."

Von Glasersfeld: Adaptation — no matter how well an individual organism feels adapted to an environment — does not produce an exact representation of the environment; such a

view is in my eyes logically false. Adaptation can only mean
that we manage to get through, that we have found a viable
course, that we do not fail. To the neurobiologist Humberto
Maturana I owe the example of the instrumental flight, which
illustrates our cognitive situation: there is the pilot in the cock-
pit, who has no access to an external world and only reacts to
what the instruments indicate. Nevertheless, pilots successfully fly and land their planes, although thunderstorms may
rage outside. The only thing they may notice of the thunderstorms is the occasional deviation of the instruments from
their course, which they then immediately correct. They identify perturbations and react accordingly. They have no idea
whatever of the actual cause, the thunderstorm, but manage to
land safely and thus to reach their goal. We can state that they
have got through. I would maintain that this situation of an
instrumental flight corresponds exactly to our relationship
with reality: we can never say what is outside the world of our
experience.

Poerksen: If science is no longer concerned with understanding an external world and with spreading the truth in an
emphatic sense, what is its task, what goal is it to serve?

Von Glasersfeld: I have the greatest respect for science but I
would like to say that it should primarily deal with the urgent
practical problems of human coexistence in our time. Here in
the United States one should, for instance, not spend billions of
dollars on particle accelerators as long as there are still people
who have to sleep in the streets, and as long as industrial
plants continue to damage and destroy the environment. I find
this absurd but such a point of view is not particularly popular
among scientists: they want to see scientific research as the
highest form of human activity, which sets its own goals and
keeps strict neutrality — no matter what happens elsewhere.

Poerksen: What specific criteria could then be laid down to
distinguish a construction of reality in the form of a scientific
theory from another? Its closeness to an imaginary pole of
truth can no longer serve as a means of distinction, if I follow
your thought.

Von Glasersfeld: The criterion that I have introduced is utility
or *viability*. I have taken the concept of viability, which is
closely related to the concept of adaptation, from the theory of

evolution. It replaces, in the world of experience, the classical philosophical notion of truth, which assumes an exact representation of reality. An organism is viable, my definition would be, if it manages to survive under given constraints and environmental conditions. And I call modes of action and thought useful or viable if they help to achieve a desired goal by overcoming all given obstacles. The assessment of the viability of a construction is, however, dependent on one's values. It contains a subjective element and requires a personal judgment. The choice of values, any ethical choice, cannot be justified by constructivism: we deal with decisions and rules that are not questionable.

Poerksen: Could you give an example of a viable theory?

Von Glasersfeld: Just think of the NASA space program; it is firmly based on Newton's formulae when satellites are launched, directed to fly around the planet Saturn, or made to land on the moon. Nevertheless, there certainly is not a single scientist among the many working for NASA who would claim that Newton's formulae, which were long ago overtaken by Albert Einstein, represented the truth. They were created for a particular purpose and they are still helpful and effective for all the relevant computations, no more and no less.

Poerksen: But how do we know, to put the question more generally, that something is useful or will prove useful in the future? This would require a prophetic gift because theories that appear viable right now may have the most terrible direct and indirect effects in the future. Therefore, we would have to integrate a *time lag* into the assessment of theories.

Von Glasersfeld: The practical implementation of a theory and its potential effects cannot always be foreseen, that is clear. I do think, however, that a scientist who spends public money is under the obligation to examine whether the theory he is working on offers *possibilities of application* that make things better or worse. Naturally, this is a relative matter and ultimately calls for a personal decision. The alternative would be an objective criterion in the sense of a representation of absolute reality; the idea would then be that science continually enlarges the domain of true knowledge, but that I consider impossible. A theory is only a model, which functions under particular circumstances — and not under others.

Poerksen: The fact, however, that the concept of viability is borrowed from the theory of evolution does suggest that it is meant to be a hard criterion for the differentiation of reality constructions. If an organism is not viable, if it cannot find a way to come to terms with the constraints of the environment, then it is, at the extreme limits, condemned to death. When a scientist formulates theories, then it is improbable that he will fail with them in a similar way.

Von Glasersfeld: Theories fail whenever observations or the results of experiments prove to be incompatible with them. False theories do not kill us, that is certainly true. But there are exceptions. The biologist and physician Alexander Bogdanov, who invented blood transfusion, proposed the theory that giving the patients a transfusion of healthy blood can cure particular diseases. Bogdanov did this once himself with a sufferer from malaria and something went wrong and both were dead within two days. But what are you driving at?

Poerksen: I want to point out that there are theories that cannot be falsified because it is, in a way, impossible to fail with them. Just think of the interpretation of a literary text, of a poem, which may lead different authors to fundamentally contradictory theories about its meaning. How would you show now which of the theories is useful and which is not?

Von Glasersfeld: This is, of course, a different area of knowledge. I would ask the persons involved in the hermeneutic activity why they are interpreting the particular poem. Are they doing it simply for their own pleasure, or do they, after all, also want to find out what other people are able to see in the text. If the latter, then we can ask: which one of two interpretations is convincing? Which of the two theories do educated readers consider more plausible? A higher measure of plausibility might be an indication of a sort of viability.

Poerksen: So now you connect, if I understand correctly, the criterion of viability with the question of intersubjective validity.

Von Glasersfeld: Right, yes. Especially with regard to the interpretation of older texts, because then we can no longer ask the authors what they really meant. Let me point out, however, that this intersubjective plausibility is also extremely important in the natural sciences. If I develop a new theory about a certain phenomenon, then it will become scientific only when others accept it. Can you remember poor old Alfred Wegener! He designed the brilliant theory of continental drift — but nobody believed him. Only years after his death, and after new observations had become available, the continental drift appeared to be a viable theory to other geologists.

The craving for stability

Poerksen: It is not yet quite clear to me what the criterion of viability primarily refers to: the explanatory power of theories; their capacity for solving problems; the ethical or unethical goals a single scientist or a group of researchers may pursue?

Von Glasersfeld: For me, the question of ethical or unethical goals is more important. However, a theory is fundamentally viable when it solves the problem in hand. Of course, scientists will not — to put it quite naively — give up their work when they are not confronted by urgent problems. There are good reasons for their carrying on: they have learned to appreciate the solving of problems, and so they will create new problems to work on in their imagination — out of curiosity, as it were. I think this is completely justified simply because they can tell themselves that one day the solution they have found for invented problems will enable them to answer those questions more quickly that have become topical in the meantime. This appears to me to be the recursive application of induction: induction means abstracting certain regularities from given experiences. Why do we do that? The reason is that such regularities seem helpful. The invention of theories is something quite similar: their construction was useful in the past — and so it appears sensible to search constantly for new questions and new answers.

Poerksen: Reducing our conversation about truth and viability to a single conclusion, I would say: there is no evidence for an approximation of ontic reality by *trial and error*.

Von Glasersfeld: Right, yes. And it is this belief, for example, that separates me from Karl Popper with whom I share many ideas otherwise. In Popper's book *Conjectures and Refutations,* there is a long and excellent chapter on instrumentalist or pragmatist philosophy, which certainly includes my sort of constructivism. It is exclusively interested in the functioning of theories and models — and not in a piecemeal approximation of truth. At the end of this chapter, Popper wants to show that instrumentalism is philosophically false and detrimental to science. But he does not succeed. He merely asserts his view but fails to provide philosophical proof for it.

Poerksen: But is Popper not right if we argue psychologically? Could we not say that instrumentalism is unsatisfactory because it disregards the fact that the search for truth is a wonderful motive for setting out on a quest that can, as we know from the beginning, never reach its end. Why labour if the conquest of truth is no longer the goal?

Von Glasersfeld: Because something much more important is at stake: surviving on our planet, for instance. As soon as we are born we want to go on living. And the question is how we can manage, despite all the constraints imposed by reality, to get through life in a reasonably satisfactory way. Whether the methods we use are true is completely irrelevant. They must only be good enough to help us reach the goals we have set ourselves.

Poerksen: Still, it cannot be denied that an emphatic, and perhaps admittedly a naive, concept of truth has stimulated human beings in most productive ways in the history of culture and science. Might this suggest that we need the idea of truth as a cognitive motive?

Von Glasersfeld: This is certainly a very tricky question. However, I do not share your view that we need the notion of truth in this connection. I much rather believe that human beings require regularities and the feeling to live in an ordered world; they need to construct causal connections and correlations, which they can project into the future. They want to maintain their stability, at any rate. The mistake is to consider such regularities as truths and to equate them with the understanding and the comprehension of the ontic world. Science and technology rest on the belief that cause-effect relations established in the past will also function in the future. David Hume already made clear that this is a necessary belief that cannot be proved: the world may very well change.

Poerksen: And the sun will not rise tomorrow morning.

Von Glasersfeld: Who can claim to know that with the kind of absolute certainty that reaches beyond past experience? It would be most embarrassing for all of us. Naturally, we hope that the sun will rise again and that we can rely on this in the future. But that is a pious hope.

Poerksen: Are you living in this spirit of fundamental uncertainty?

Von Glasersfeld: As far as everyday life is concerned, it is undoubtedly an advantage to be able to rely on assumed regularities and long-established arrangements. It is not as if I would open the door of my house to check whether the balcony is still there before I step out. I simply take for granted that it has not vanished, I open the door and step out without hesitation. It has worked all right so far — but it is not absolute knowledge.

Sharpening the sense of the possible

Poerksen: What about the sphere of thinking and the system of personal beliefs? Can one live in the awareness here that everything could at any time be different?

Von Glasersfeld: For my part, I think it has enormous advantages to be aware of the relativity of one's own constructions. Everything becomes easier. Take a trivial example: in the USA, many people believe that one must own a car and a fridge in order to be happy. And one day these people may be upset by the fact that they can no longer afford the car that is supposed to guarantee their life's happiness. Then such a fixation and rigidity, such one-way thinking, will block other paths and create unhappiness. This is to mean: the constructivist view — at least in my experience — opens up possibilities of existence that previously seemed unthinkable.

Poerksen: The writer Robert Musil, in a similar vein, speaks of *the unwritten poem of my own existence* and the *sharpening of the sense of the possible.*

Von Glasersfeld: That is splendid and suits me perfectly. This poem of possibilities must always be kept an open option. Every fixation and decision may mean the elimination of possibilities meriting special consideration. However, it would be foolish to believe that we could simply clear away our beliefs — and then construct the desired and longed-for world at pleasure.

Poerksen: What is the framework within which we may invent ourselves?

Von Glasersfeld: The world is the sum of the constraints impinging on our personalities, our plans, and movements. What manifests itself here is a cybernetic principle: cybernetics does not work — as already pointed out by Gregory Bateson — with causal relations but with constraints. That is the point: we must lead our lives within these constraints, and we should not view our plans to achieve some future goals as the only possibility and try to implement them regardless of the given constraints.

Poerksen: At what point does the world react against the imposition of our constructions? In what moment do the objects scream "No!" when they are to be locked away in a classified drawer of thoughts?

Von Glasersfeld: I would say that it is not a question of objects. The ability to speak of objects presupposes a structure and certain relationships with other objects. What you are calling the world of objects appears to me more like an amorphous whirling that is, however, so multifarious that we are able to create constant models by means of the internal correlation of sensations. Inside us the summing of continual neuronal activities constantly generates combinations of impulses from which we then construct our world.

Poerksen: How can one, from this point of view, distinguish between illusion and reality, right and wrong? How can you do this as a scientist without falling back on the emphatic idea of truth rejected before?

Von Glasersfeld: In everyday life this is rarely a problem. When someone proposes a theory about the mounting of car tyres without the use of a jack, then we can try it out — and I can say to them: "Let's do it!" In all practical matters viability can, in principle, be established experimentally. The main concern of science is to engineer this kind of proof: a theory is proposed; its utility must be examined; experiments are invented to test it.

Poerksen: This sounds rather unglamorous because all it means is: the constructivist abandons any exaggerated claim to the knowledge of truth — and then carries on as before. The posture revealed by your statements does not seem to do justice to the more or less direct promise of innovation for which constructivism is celebrated today.

Von Glasersfeld: You are referring to the expectations of certain people; they have nothing to do with me. Why should I consider myself responsible for such expectations? Sorry, but this is not my problem. Radical constructivism, for me, is a thoroughly practical and prosaic matter; all it offers is a potentially useful mode of thinking, nothing more. It is most important to keep in mind from the beginning to the end that constructivism, too, is only a model. Whether it is a viable model of thinking or whether it seems practicable to people cannot be determined for everybody and all times; each and every individual must find out for him- or herself.

The linguistic world-view

Poerksen: How did you discover this utility for yourself? Let me speculate: looking at your biography and roughly reconstructing its external stages makes me think that the viability of constructivism and the relativity of reality must have been formative life experiences for you. You grew up in the South Tyrol, studied mathematics in Zurich and Vienna, were a skiing instructor in Australia, a farmer in Ireland, a journalist and translator in Italy, and a professor of cognitive psychology in the USA.

Von Glasersfeld: There is an intimate connection between my life and the constructivist insights — you are quite right there. The mere fact that I grew up with more than one language, that I did not only speak but live in these languages, rendered the idea of one reality problematic. I learned German, English, and Italian in the environment of my childhood. I was taught excellent French in a Swiss boarding school but only learned to understand and really incorporate it when I lived in Paris for a year. It soon struck me that the world was different depending on whether I spoke French, English, German, or Italian.

Poerksen: Do you take the view that every language shapes and structures the experience of reality?

Von Glasersfeld: I think that this thesis must be formulated more prudently and more precisely. Children realise right at the beginning of their lives that they can achieve an enormous amount by uttering sounds, that sounds may be a most powerful instrument. But they also realise that it is very difficult to learn the proper use of this instrument. We are not equipped with a plan at the beginning of our lives that would explain all possible meanings, but we are forced to learn from situations and to explore language by using it. The application of every single word is accompanied by wrong inferences; and only gradually and in a long drawn-out process we are able to patch together the meanings of our own words. And the meaning associated with a sound or a letter finally results from the experiences we make in interactive situations with other speakers. When I live among Italians I am made aware of a particular way of viewing and analysing the world. Sharing experiences with English people at the same time makes me realise immediately that there are marked differences between these two languages. The Italians and the English may both believe that their languages represent the world in the appropriate way. Living between these two languages and worlds, as I do, I can only affirm the insurmountable subjectivity of word meanings and point out the characteristic difference in the representations of reality. From this experience of my life stems my interest in what is called reality.

Poerksen: Could you quote an example illustrating the diversity of world views underlying their linguistic representations?

Von Glasersfeld: Just think of prepositions and the characteristic relationships they can generate within a language. Translating a couple of sentences from English into German, for instance, may involve the proper rendering of conceptual relationships expressed by prepositions. And then we notice immediately that these two languages, which are not very far apart historically, do not match. The German preposition *in* includes at least 30 spatial, temporal, and modal relations. The English *in* is no less powerful but some of the relations it represents are different. (*I say it in English* becomes "Ich sage es auf deutsch"; *in my place* becomes "an meiner Stelle"; *in this way* becomes "auf diese Weise" etc.). Consider how often prepositions like *in, on, after, over* etc. are used, and how important they are because they constitute relationships between objects and situations, and you will realise that there are all sorts of relations and loose associations in a language, which do not match those in another.

Poerksen: What you have presented nicely illustrates the so-called "linguistic relativity principle" formulated by Benjamin Lee Whorf in his famous article *Linguistics as an exact science.* He wrote: "… users of markedly different grammars are pointed by their grammars toward different types of observations and different evaluations of externally similar acts of observation, and hence are not equivalent as observers but must arrive at somewhat different views of the world."

Von Glasersfeld: Exactly, that is quite correct. The diversity of the perceptions of reality is what one experiences when living in more than one language. Here is a little story about a relevant experience of mine. A friend from England once visited me in Milan. We went on an excursion and wandered along a river when we reached a spot where the railway line joined the river. In the meadow near the riverbank, quite close to the rail track, an Italian family was sitting enjoying a picnic. Suddenly we heard the distant rumble of the approaching train; the mother jumped up and shouted: "Attenti bambini, arriva il treno." My English friend turned to me: "What did she say?" And I realised that I could not simply give a literal translation of this sentence; it had to be: "Be careful, children, the train is *coming*" — and not: "Be careful, children, the train is *arriving.*" The reason is that the verb *to arrive* presupposes a stationary element; the train must stop. In Italian, you can use *arrivare* to express that something is in the process of approaching.

Poerksen: Becoming aware of this fundamental diversity in the meanings of expressions and realising that even in one single language different group-specific semantic systems exist side by side, the communicative situations we have to take into account appear most complicated. The question is then: What does it mean to understand an utterance if the meanings of expressions, as you maintain, are essentially subjective and differ from language to language?

Von Glasersfeld: In my view, it is impossible to expect that a person's utterance activates precisely the same thoughts and conceptual networks that the person originally associated with it. This is to say: *transmission, message,* and *receiver* are misleading metaphors with respect to conceptual content. *Communication is never transport.* What moves from one human being to another are sounds, graphic figures or, as in telegraphy, electric impulses — in brief, oscillating patterns of sound, light or electricity. And we can only assign meanings to these energy changes in terms of our own linguistic experiences. Ever so often we speak with people and realise two or three days later that they have not understood at all what we meant to say or thought we said.

Poerksen: We never know whether we understand each other?

Von Glasersfeld: No, we can never be sure because there is no possibility of control and inspection. I can never really know what goes on in somebody else's head; I can only go by what they say — and what generates certain ideas in my head that are themselves the products of individual and subjective experiences. The feeling of understanding results, I think, because the other person does not do or say anything that might indicate an incorrect interpretation on my part.

Poerksen: Does this mean that we recognise failed communication only when we in fact notice that we quite definitely do *not* understand each other?

Von Glasersfeld: That is how it is. That we failed to understand each other I can only effectively ascertain when the other person says or does something that is, in my view, incompatible with what I said. However, the fact that societies and environments are comparatively similar justifies our expectation that the people we talk to understand the words that we use in a similar way or at least interpret them in a way that does not contradict our own interpretations. Consequently, the vagueness of the meanings of expressions is significantly restricted.

The end of instruction

Poerksen: During the last few years, you have published a great number of articles dealing with the principles of constructivist didactics. Your reflections on the act of understanding and the viability of constructivism are a good point of departure, I think, to illustrate the practical import of your thinking with reference to the field of education. Let me put the question quite generally: What consequences for schools can be derived from your epistemological considerations?

Von Glasersfeld: The first consequence from what has been said so far is nearly trivial: language cannot be used to transfer conceptual content; all conceptual content must be constructed by the students themselves. The compulsion to learn things by rote, constant repetition, and other forms of dressage cannot guarantee understanding.

Poerksen: Are not the favourable school reports, which the children bring home, an indication that they have understood what they were taught?

Von Glasersfeld: Well, we simply need good reports and good marks in order to be upgraded. But they are, of course, not unambiguous indicators of students' understanding of a subject, of whether, for example, they are really capable of applying some formula from physics. Despite good marks, they often lack the insight into how the conceptual connections between the symbols in a formula must be understood.

Poerksen: What other insights can constructivism supply for education?

Von Glasersfeld: From a constructivist point of view, it seems most important to me to take students seriously as intelligent beings capable of independent thinking, that is to say, as beings that construct their own reality. Students are neither idiots nor victims to be filled with knowledge. The respect I am demanding here is justified by the fact that it is the students who, in the process of learning, construct knowledge actively and on the basis of what they already know. It is therefore indispensable, I believe, that teachers build up at least approximate images of what goes on in the minds of their students; in this way only, they will stand a chance of changing something there. This means that everything children say and do must be taken seriously as an expression of their thinking.

Poerksen: Even when children utter patently meaningless or incorrect things?

Von Glasersfeld: Most children's utterances are not at all meaningless — they are only incomprehensible to us adults, at first. We must ask ourselves: Why is this or that utterance meaningful *for the child*? How is that possible? — The "mistakes" of students are, therefore, of enormous importance: they provide insights into their thinking, and they offer decisive hints for the creation of new situations in which the faulty solutions and methods of the children will no longer work. This is the best way for inducing what Jean Piaget called *accommodation*: if the results of one's actions do not match one's expectations, then learning can begin.

Poerksen: Listening to what you are saying makes me understand one of the inspired exaggerations voiced by the communication scientist Gordon Pask: he proposes that the students become the teachers. Teachers have to learn from students what the students do not know and why they have difficulties to grasp and apply what they are told.

Von Glasersfeld: The statement by Gordon Pask that you quote is not too much of an exaggeration. In middle school, at the latest, teachers can really learn from their students because the students may hit upon ideas unknown to the teachers. Some of the children with whom I worked in mathematics classes managed to invent clever methods of subtraction that, however, functioned only in the precisely delimited area of the problem configuration in hand. They could not be generalised. Nevertheless, it is quite conceivable that teachers can profit enormously from students; they may get to know tricks that students have managed to contrive because they have perceived their tasks from an unprejudiced point of view.

Poerksen: For many people, however, the static culture of instruction, which secures the maximal authority of the teachers, is definitely more attractive.

Von Glasersfeld: Go and talk to teachers who have been teaching for 15 or 20 years. Of course, I do not know the situation in Germany, but in the USA you will encounter many soured and desperate people who know that what they are doing does not work. Whenever teachers are successfully brought to observe constructivist methods in their schools and really attend to them, they are forced to acknowledge that something different and something new is happening there: the children become active; they even show signs of pleasure; they enjoy their time in class because there is no fixed curriculum; and they love doing something when they are not compelled to do it.

Poerksen: But this different manner of teaching would possibly use up too much time, time that simply is not available. Some teachers probably fear that the children — if dealt with according to these ideas — would not learn enough of all that which they simply have to learn, too.

Von Glasersfeld: It is the job of teachers to be patient. Naturally, adapting to constructivistically inspired teaching will cost time, but applying these considerations continually will often produce something astonishing. It may happen that children approach their teachers after class and ask for further tasks. Manners begin to change; children realise that it is enjoyable and satisfying to solve problems. Fortunately, there are now quite a few empirical investigations that confirm the success of constructivist methods in mathematics teaching. They show that children at the end of their first year are just about equally good as the children taught in the conventional way. At the end of the second year they are better, statistically. And in their third year it becomes apparent that they have learnt how to learn: they are now superior to their contemporaries also in other subjects because their whole attitude towards school and the taught subjects has changed.

Poerksen: The constructivist premise of the impossibility of absolute truth also implies, it seems to me, the teaching of even the *hard sciences* as historical disciplines. In concrete terms: mention Democritus when talking about atoms, Faraday in connection with electricity, and link optical phenomena with the historical ideas about vision and visual perception that reach back into antiquity. And so on. Students would always, in a more or less direct way, be enlightened about the historical conditions of the origin and the relativity of what passes for knowledge.

Von Glasersfeld: A wonderful idea that, however, meets with aggressive resistance from certain quarters. I have often spoken at conferences of the *International Association of the History and Philosophy of Science in Science Teaching*; the relativisation of scientific knowledge appeared to many teachers who were attending these conferences, an intolerable idea that undermined their position of authority. I would therefore recommend that these teachers no longer base their authority on the quantity of apparently objective knowledge but on their capability and experience in solving problems together with their students. What must be thrown out unconditionally is the notion that teachers are omniscient. This is my recommendation.

From outsider philosophy to fashion

Poerksen: Leaving questions of education again and surveying the whole situation of constructivism we cannot fail to notice that, from the perspective of the history of knowledge, constructivism has entered an explosive phase. It is in the process of being transformed from an outsider philosophy into a fashion, and in certain publications it even assumes the traits of a *weltanschauung*. Did you ever expect this kind of popularisation and transformation of your ideas?

Von Glasersfeld: Not in my wildest dreams would I have thought that constructivism would be received in this way. The possibility of a transformation of these ideas into an intellectual fashion never occurred to me; but there is nothing one can do about it. What people do with certain ideas is their business. True enough, an uncanny number of people call themselves constructivists today. At home there are many who have no idea whatever of the basic tenets of constructivism. My only hope is that these ideas will open up a more advantageous view of the world for some people. And this hope outweighs the misunderstandings, the trappings of fashion, and the innumerable abounding misconceptions. They seem to me less important.

Poerksen: In what ways is constructivism helpful for you personally? Can it possibly prepare for the inevitability of disease and pain?

Von Glasersfeld: But of course. Perhaps I am a bit naive in this regard but constructivism has made many things clear to me. If I can, in principle, never truly know the reality beyond the experiential world of my life, then it is meaningless to worry about what may happen or perhaps not happen when my time in this experiential world is ending. It seems totally meaningless to me to be afraid of death; I am afraid of pain, of falling over and fracturing my bones. It happened last year, and it was painful; but that is something entirely different. And it is certainly imaginable that I will be struck by sentimental feelings of nostalgia one day, when I have to accept that I cannot cultivate my habits any more. But I do not know how I came into my world; I do know that my time in this world is limited. Why should I worry?

The knowledge of knowledge entails responsibility

Humberto R. Maturana on truth and oppression, structure determinism and dictatorship, and the autopoiesis of living

© Michael Heitmann / Hamburg

Humberto R. Maturana, (b. 1928) first studied medicine in Chile, then anatomy in England, was awarded a Ph.D. in biology at Harvard in 1958, and subsequently worked at the Massachusetts Institute of Technology (MIT). In 1960, he returned to work with the University of Chile at Santiago, which he only left for occasion periods of research and teaching abroad. He is particularly well known for his theory of autopoiesis (self-creation) that he began to develop in the late 1960s. This theory provides a novel feature of living beings going beyond the traditional criteria of biology – reproduction, mobility, etc.   According to Maturana, a circular, autopoietic form of organisation distinguishes living beings, from the amoeba to humans. Living systems form a network of internal and circularly enmeshed processes of production that make them bounded unities by constantly producing and thus maintaining themselves. Autopoietic systems are autonomous. Whatever may happen inside them, whatever may penetrate and stimulate, perturb or destroy them, is essentially determined by their own circular organisation.

At the beginning of the 1970s, Maturana further elaborated the theory of autopoiesis together with the biologist Francisco J. Varela, who was then also teaching in Chile. They cooperated with systems theorists and politicians who, on the initiative of the newly elected socialist president Salvador Allende, had been engaged to reorganise the communication systems and the economy of the Republic. In 1973, the dictator Pinochet seized power and destroyed, amongst other things, the existing university environment. Numerous professors were dismissed and driven out; many were murdered or deported. Despite repeated threats from the side of the regime, Maturana stayed in Chile. The concept of autopoiesis began to gain greater popularity in the early 1980s. In the meantime, it has exploded in academic circles and become a synonym for an autonomous form of reality production. It has taken on a vital life of its own as a universally exploitable trendy concept in journals on systems thinking and family therapy or at the conferences of sociologists and media scholars — even in the face of resistance by its creator.

Humberto R. Maturana is still active as a professor of biology who seeks to promote a theory of cognition in the context of the natural sciences. Until his retirement, he was director of the Laboratory for Experimental Epistemology and the Biology of Cognition at the University of Chile in Santiago, which he had founded himself.

The explanation of experience

Poerksen: You once said that *truth* and *reality* often serve as motives for violence. How are we to understand this?

Maturana: We live in a culture that does not respect differences but only tolerates them. So just because certain people think that they are in the possession of truth, the situation frequently arises that everything unfamiliar and extraordinary will appear as an unacceptable and insupportable threat. The possible consequence of such an attitude is that people feel justified to use violence because they claim to have privileged access to *reality* or to *the truth,* or to fight for a great ideal. This attitude, so they believe, justifies their behaviour and sets them apart from common criminals.

Poerksen: Who is the target of this criticism of an idea of truth turned totalitarian? Where do you see such forms of conflict?

Maturana: They are ubiquitous although they need not always end in physical threats towards other people. In political and polemical debates, which are often similar to fights or even wars, we reject other people and their views. We attack them without listening, in fact, we refuse to listen because we are so very sure that they hold views that are patently false. Political terrorism rests on the idea that certain people are wrong and must, therefore, be killed.

Poerksen: This might mean that any idea of truth necessarily leads to violence. Would you accept that? Or, to reverse the question: Is there not a less dangerous and less fanatical way of handling the view that one has discovered the reality of the world as it is?

Maturana: It all depends on the emotions of the people relating to each other. If they respect each other, then the fact that they hold different views may offer the opportunity of a fruitful conversation and a productive exchange. If people, however, do not respect each other but demand subservience, then their differing views will engender motives for negation.

Poerksen: Reading your books or listening to you talking gives me the impression that you have invented a new theory of truth. Philosophers speaking about truth have always asked the question: How does truth come about? Truth seemed to them to be the result of some social convention (consensus theory of truth), the result of some experience of immediate evidence (evidence theory of truth), or the product of a correspondence between theory and reality (correspondence theory of truth). You do not ask how truth comes about but seek to develop what I would call a *consequence theory of truth*. The question now is: What are the consequences of the idea of truth? How does the atmosphere of a conversation change if notions of truth start to dominate it?

Maturana: I hold a different view. It is not my goal to create a new theory of truth. I am concerned with something that is of much more fundamental importance: The classic inquiries into truth, reality, or the essence of being, deal with truth, reality and being as something independent from, and external to, an observer. My key questions are: How can experience be explained? How can I do what I am doing right now? How do I operate as an observer? What criterion am I using to justify that what I am saying is in fact the case? Such a view of things changes the whole traditional system of questions centred on the validation of an external reality or truth — and the observer moves into focus. We no longer occupy ourselves with the assumed properties of an external reality or truth but we begin to understand the references to *the reality* or *the truth* as the proposal of an explanation by an observer who is telling us about his experiences. I do not presuppose reality as given in my work.

Poerksen: What does this mean? In what sense are reality and truth attempted explanations?

Maturana: They are explanatory proposals to eliminate doubt. If you refer to reality and truth in this way, you need no longer deal with the problem of how you know what you are asserting. What you know simply derives from what there is, from a connection with reality. When we say that we are absolutely sure of something, we mean that we are no longer forced to reflect, to ask questions, and to entertain doubts.

Poerksen: So you are not concerned with questions of truth and the opposition *true-false* but with the distinction between two fundamentally different positions: you either assert that all cognition is observer-dependent, or you assert that an observer-independent reality can be perceived.

Maturana: You could put it that way, yes. I am not interested in the question as to whether an observer-independent reality exists and whether I or somebody else may know it. I use the observer as the starting-point of my thinking, avoiding any ontological assumption, simply out of curiosity and interest in the questions involved. There is no higher reason, no ontological foundation, no universally valid justification for these questions. Observers observe, see something, affirm or deny its existence, and do whatever they do. Without the observer, there is nothing. The observer is the foundation of all knowledge, of any assumption involving the human self, the world and the cosmos. The disappearance of the observer would mean the end and the disappearance of the world we know; there would be nobody left to perceive, to speak, to describe, and to explain. What exists independently from this observer is necessarily and inevitably a matter of belief and not of secure knowledge because to see something always requires someone who sees it. The observer and the operation of observing are my topics of research and, at the same time, its objective and its instrument. I do not start with ontology, I start with experience. Here I am, Humberto Maturana, reflecting and posing the reflexive question how it is possible for me to reflect and to know how I know. And then I am confronted by the inescapable conclusion that I have to deal with biology: the scientist facing this question, the philosopher, the mathematician, the priest, the burglar, the politician — they are all human beings, living and structure-determined systems, biological entities.

Poerksen: Who is, in fact, an observer? What do observers do?

Maturana: Human beings — beings who live in language — operate as observers when they, acting in self-awareness, use a distinction in order to distinguish something. They are aware of seeing and perceiving something. Somebody who is simply looking out of the window I would not consider an observer.

Poerksen: The ability to observe is tied to the possibility of self-reflection.

Maturana: And this self-reflection and thinking about what we are doing takes place in language. Suppose we both watch a bird eating a worm or some other insect. When we ask ourselves whether the bird knows that it is eating a worm, we perform an operation in language that is unavailable to the bird because it does not live in language. The bird does not produce comments that serve to reflect its actions. It is therefore not an observer. It simply eats a worm — and we human beings observe its behaviour.

Poerksen: Do you separate the observer from the observed? Do you work with the traditional distinction between subject and object?

Maturana: The act of distinction consists in operating in such a manner as to produce something that seems to be independent from one's own person. Now, it has become accepted in our culture to distinguish between the observer and the observed, as if there were a difference between the two, as if they were distinct. If this is assumed and accepted, we are immediately confronted by the task of describing the relation between these two supposedly independent entities with greater precision. I do not myself work with this classic distinction between observers and observed but I show how that which is distinguished is connected with the persons performing the distinction, and to what extent observers are involved in the distinctions they actually perform. My central point of departure is the experience of a human being. How come that we can speak about things and objects as if they were independent from us? This is what I want to find out.

Poerksen: What are the consequences of learning to understand that we are observers in this sense, of becoming aware that we ourselves actually create particular distinctions and write them into the world?

Maturana: Becoming aware that one is doing the observing, and then being aware of being aware that it is oneself who makes the distinctions, one attains a new domain of experience. Becoming aware of one's awareness and understanding one's understanding gives rise to the feeling of responsibility for what one is doing, for what one is creating through one's own operations of distinction. This kind of insight has something inevitable: once this has been understood, one cannot pretend any longer to be unaware of one's own understanding if one is actually aware of it and is also aware of this awareness. Even those who deny this kind of awareness are ineluctably aware of it: for acting hypocritically and lying implies asserting something that contradicts one's own insights. This is why I wrote in the last chapter of the book *The tree of knowledge* that it is not understanding that entails responsibility but the knowledge of knowledge.

Poerksen: Your key concept of the *observer* seems to me to be a somewhat unfortunate choice to express what you intend to say? In ordinary language, it signals separation: we observe, keep a distance, and indirectly insist on neutrality. Would it not be better to replace observers by *participants* or *sharers* who are inseparably tied to their worlds and who massively contribute to the production and construction of these worlds?

Maturana: I am not at all unhappy with the concept of the observer, definitely not, because it actually invites us to explain the experience of observing: the table and the chairs in this room, my jacket, the scarf I am wearing — all these things appear to me to have an existence of their own that is independent from me. The problem that should not be made invisible by a concept like *participation* is the following: How do I know that these things are there? What kind of assertion do I make when I say that the world unfolding before my eyes in all its beauty exists independently from me? Your suggestion to speak of a sharer or participant is misleading because the notion of participation already contains an explanation and a ready-made answer; the only admissible question left would then concern the specific manner in which the assumed participation is realised. Observing is an experience which also has to do with the apparently independent existence of things, and that has to be explained. The concept of the observer is a challenge to study the operation of observing and to face up to the circularity of the understanding of understanding. It is, after all, an observer who observes the observing and strives to explain it; it is a brain that wants to explain the brain. Many people think that such reflexive problems are unacceptable and unsolvable. My proposal, however, is to accept this circular situation fully right from the start and to make oneself the instrument by means of which the question of one's personal experience and one's own actions is to be answered through one's very own activities. The point is to observe the operations, which give rise to the experiences that are to be explained.

Fear of madness

Poerksen: Your plea for circular thinking somehow seems deeply disturbing, even threatening. The world dissolves; beginning and end become arbitrary fixations no longer offering a safe grip; all firm ground is pulled from under our feet. One would like to rush to the door and out of the room, but one has become uncertain that that door is still there. You reported somewhere that, having started to think in this way, you were quite scared for some time that you might go mad. Why did that alarm finally fade away?

Maturana: There came a moment at which I realised that circular thinking did not endanger the soundness of my mind but that it expanded my understanding. The decision, in particular, to proceed from my own experience and not from an external reality can have a profoundly liberating and comforting effect. The experiences we make are no longer doubted, no longer denigrated as unreal and illusory; they are no longer a problem, they no longer produce emotional conflicts; they are simply accepted for what they are. – Suppose, I claim to have heard the voice of Jesus speaking to me last night. What do you think would happen when I told other people of such an experience? Somebody might explain to me that I suffered from hallucinations because Jesus was dead and could therefore not possibly speak to me. Someone else might think me very vain and suspect that I wanted to present myself as an elect person: it is, after all, Jesus who was speaking to me. A third person might say that during that night the devil had led me into temptation. All these considerations have one thing in common: they reject the explanation with which I am trying to make sense of my experience but they do not negate the experience itself; they do not call into question that I heard a voice.

Poerksen: In what way does this example contribute to answering my question concerning your fear of madness? I assume that your principled decision to start out from your own experience allayed your fears, calmed your mind, and set you at ease. One accepts what one experiences. Therefore, the fear of madness might be a sort of clandestine attempt to defend oneself against one's own experiences.

Maturana: This is the point. To call something *mad* means to explain one's perceptions and experiences in such a way as to devalue oneself. It is not my intention to reject or devalue experiences. Once again: experiences are never the problem. What I want to explain is the operations through which experiences arise.

Poerksen: Do you believe that such a view, which so forcefully argues in favour of the legitimacy of any kind of experience, offers ethical advantages?

Maturana: Yes, I do. We must not forget that the notion of a reality existing independently from us corresponds with the belief that it is possible to achieve authoritative, universally valid statements. These may then be used to discredit certain kinds of experience. It is the reference to this reality that is held to make a statement universally valid; in a culture based on power, domination, and control, it provides the justification for forcing other people to subject themselves to one's own view of things. However, as soon as one has realised that there is no single privileged access to reality, and that perception and illusion are indistinguishable in the actual process of an experience, then the question arises what criteria are used by a human being to claim that something is the case. The very possibility of posing this question opens up a space of common reflection, a sphere of cooperation. The other person becomes a legitimate counterpart with whom I am able to talk. Friendship, mutual respect, and cooperation emerge. It is no longer possible to demand submission; the universe changes into a multiverse within which numerous realities are valid by reference to different criteria of validity. The only thing one may now do is to invite the other person to think about what one believes and holds to be valid oneself.

I think we may sensibly distinguish between two distinct attitudes, two paths of thinking and explaining. The first path I call *objectivity without parentheses*. It takes for granted the observer-independent existence of objects that can be known; it believes in the possibility of an external validation of statements. Such a validation would lend authority and unconditional legitimacy to what is claimed and would, therefore, aim at submission. It entails the negation of all those who are not prepared to agree with the "objective" facts. One does not want to listen to them or try to understand them. The fundamental emotion reigning here is powered by the authority of universally valid knowledge.

The other attitude I call *objectivity in parentheses;* its emotional basis is the enjoyment of the company of other human beings. The question of the observer is accepted fully, and every attempt is made to answer it. The distinction of objects is, according to this path, not denied but the reference to objects is not the basis of explanations, it is the coherence of experiences with other experiences that constitutes the foundation of all explanation. In this view, the observer becomes the origin of all realities; all realities are created through the observer's operations of distinction. If we follow this path of explanation, we become aware that we can in no way claim to be in possession of *the truth* but that there are numerous possible realities. Each of them is fully legitimate and valid although, of course, not equally desirable. If we follow this path of explanation, we cannot demand the submission of our fellow human beings but will listen to them, seek cooperation and conversation.

Principles of aesthetic seduction

Poerksen: Such acceptance of the other could be most helpful, I believe, to pull the rug from underneath the innumerable quarrels in the microcosms of private lives and in the macrocosms of public spaces. For me, the question is now how we might promote and practise this very fundamental kind of respect in a manner that does not in any way involve domination. If you want to remain consistent, you surely cannot force other people to agree to your thoughts. How are we to proceed, then, if dominance and manipulation are inadmissible? How do you convince people?

Maturana: I never attempt to convince anyone. The only thing left for me to do is to converse with those people who seek and wish to converse with me. I give lectures if people want to listen to me; I write articles and books and work with my students. And one day perhaps a young man comes to Chile from Germany to visit me and asks for more precise details.

Poerksen: In the last passages of your famous paper *Biology of Cognition* you outline the concept of *aesthetic seduction*. What does this mean? How can one use the aesthetic to convince in an appealing manner?

Maturana: The idea of aesthetic seduction is based on the insight that people enjoy beauty. We call something *beautiful* when the circumstances we find ourselves in make us feel well. Judging something as *ugly* and *unpleasant,* on the other hand, indicates displeasure because we are aware of the difference to our views of what is agreeable and pleasant. The aesthetic is harmony and pleasure, the enjoyment of what is given to us. An attractive view transforms us. A beautiful picture makes us look at it again and again, enjoy its colour scheme, photograph it, perhaps even buy it. In brief, the relationship with a picture may transform the life of people because the picture has become a source of aesthetic experience.

Poerksen: It would interest me to know what this idea of aesthetic seduction means to you when you write, give lectures or interviews. Although this sounds like probing for rhetorical tricks and manipulation, I would like to know what you are, in fact, doing when you try to seduce people.

Maturana: I certainly never intend to seduce or persuade people in a manipulative way. Beauty would vanish if I tried to seduce in this way. Any attempt to persuade applies pressure and destroys the possibility of listening. Pressure creates resentment. Wanting to manipulate people stimulates resistance. Manipulation means to exploit our relation with other people in such a way as to give them the impression that whatever happens is beneficial and advantageous to them. But the resulting actions of the manipulated person are, in fact, useful for the manipulator. Manipulation, therefore, really means cheating people. No, the only thing left to me in the way of aesthetic seduction is just to be what I am, wholly and entirely, and to admit no discrepancy whatsoever between what I am saying and what I am doing. Of course, this does not at all exclude some jumping about and playacting during a lecture. But not in order to persuade or to seduce but in order to generate the experiences that produce and make manifest what I am talking about. The persons becoming acquainted with me in this way can then decide for themselves whether they want to accept what they see before them. Only when there is no discrepancy between what is said and what is done, when there is no pretence and no pressure, aesthetic seduction may unfold. In such a situation, the people listening and debating will feel accepted in such measure as to be able to present themselves in an uninhibited and pleasurable manner. They are not attacked, they are not forced to do things, and they can show themselves as they are, because someone else is presenting himself naked and unprotected. Such behaviour is always seductive in a respectful way because all questions and fears suddenly become legitimate and completely new possibilities of encountering one another emerge. I think people realise immediately when something is wrong: they are experts in detecting hypocrisy.

Poerksen: Let us assume that someone categorically refused to listen to you and to follow your thoughts. What would happen then?

Maturana: What could happen then? That is all perfectly legitimate. In some of my lectures I mention that I have added three further rights to the United Nations catalogue of human rights: the right to make mistakes; the right to change one's view; and the right to leave the room at any moment. If people are allowed to make mistakes, they can correct them. People who are entitled to change their views can reflect. If people have the right to get up and leave at any moment, they will stay only if they wish to.

The salamander and the internal construction of the world

Poerksen: It may be useful at this point to recall some of your fundamental ideas in order to move on to another topic. You say that all knowledge is necessarily observer-dependent; that absolute reality assertions lead to terror, and that any form of coercion must be rejected. My impression is that all the ideas we have been discussing so far involve ethical assumptions in a very wide sense. We have been talking about conclusions and consequences relating to the claim that objective knowledge is impossible. My question is now whether your ethical demands can be justified epistemologically. Is there evidence for the impossibility of objective knowledge of the world? Is there proof?

Maturana: Answering your question requires the clarification of what we want to accept as proof. We must first establish what it really means to say that something is true or false? Is a hypothesis proved because it fits into what I am thinking? Am I perhaps prepared to listen and to trust the method of proof simply because of this correspondence between the so-called evidence and my own presuppositions? Do we therefore call something false because it is not in harmony with our preconceptions? Can something be false or right *per se*? What are the criteria used by people to accept some assertion as proven? My own answer to these questions is that I am a scientist who is able to state the conditions under which something happens that I claim is actually happening. What I am saying is neither *true* nor *false*.

Poerksen: In your books you describe experiments with frogs, salamanders, and pigeons. You studied perception in these animals; your epistemological insights are, as I understand you, the products of your work in the laboratory. Do these studies merely illustrate the assumption, which is unprovable in principle, that we can never know the real world, or is there more to them?

Maturana: These experiments relate to my personal history and my experiences as a scientist; they must not be taken as evidence or indications of truth; they outline and describe the points of departure and the course of my own way of thinking. When I speak about the experiments with frogs, pigeons or salamanders I refer to the circumstances in which my ideas developed over time. In this way, the conditions are revealed that induced me to leave the traditional paths of perception research and to change the established system of epistemological inquiry.

Poerksen: Could you exemplify the history of your re-orientation by some relevant experiment?

Maturana: Let me select a number of experiments carried out by the American biologist Roger Sperry in the early 1940ies. Roger Sperry removed one of the eyes of a salamander, severed the optic nerve, rotated the eye by 180 degrees, and carefully put it back into its socket. The optic nerve regenerated and the vision of the rotated eyes in the animals returned after some time. Everything healed but there was a crucial difference: the salamanders threw their tongue with a deviation of 180 degrees, when they wanted to catch a worm. The extent of the deviation corresponded exactly to the degree of rotation performed on the eyes. With these experiments, Roger Sperry wanted to find out whether the optic nerve was capable of regenerating and whether the fibres of the optic nerve would re-grow to join their original projection areas in the brain. The answer is: that is indeed what happens. He also wanted to find out whether the salamanders are able to correct their behaviour — whether they would manage to hit the worm again with their tongue. The answer here is: no, that is not possible; the animals keep tonguing with a deviation of 180 degrees; they starve to death if they are not fed. When I myself heard about these experiments I began to realise, however, that Roger Sperry had formulated a misleading question that tended to obscure the observed phenomenon.

The hidden epistemology of the experiment

Poerksen: In what respect was his research goal misleading?

Maturana: Roger Sperry started out from the assumption that the salamander aims at a worm in the external world with his tongue. His question implied, as Gregory Bateson would have said, a whole epistemology. It takes for granted implicitly that the external object is processed in the brain of the salamander in the form of information about its shape and location. The salamander, consequently, makes a mistake; it does not process the information coming from outside correctly. However, I found it much more meaningful to interpret the experiment in a completely different way. The salamander, I claimed, correlates the activities of the motor apparatus of its tongue with the activities of its retina. If its retina shows the image of a worm, it throws out its tongue; it does not aim at a worm in the external world. The correlation given in this case is an internal one. Seen in this way, it is not at all surprising that it does not change its behaviour.

Poerksen: How did you yourself discover the hidden epistemology of this experiment? And what experiences and observations have led you from the experiment to an empirical epistemology?

Maturana: When I performed experiments on the colour perception of pigeons, I proceeded from assumptions quite similar to those made by Roger Sperry. My goal was to show how the colours in the external world, which I had specified in terms of their spectral composition, are correlated with the activities in the retina. I wanted to establish the connections between Red, Green and Blue and the activities of the retina, i.e. the retinal ganglion cells. What did the red, green, or blue objects release?

Poerksen: So you thought likewise that the external object determines what happens inside the organism.

Maturana: Quite right. But one day it dawned upon me that the correlation I was looking for could in all probability never be established. Perhaps I should, I said to myself, deal with the question whether the activity of the retina could be shown to be connected with the names of colours. The consequence was a momentous change with regard to the goal of my research.

Suddenly I found myself outside the established traditions of perception research.

Poerksen: This does indeed sound somewhat strange. Names and designations of colours or whatever are, after all, merely arbitrary, merely conventional.

Maturana: True. People naturally thought I was crazy. The colour terms, however, do say something about the persons who have particular experiences, they are indicators of experiences, they point to experiences. What I had to demonstrate, therefore, was that the activities of the retina are correlated with the specific experiences represented by colour names. That is precisely what I managed to show in one of my studies. A colour is, to pursue the thought further, nothing external but something happening in an organism — merely released by an external source of light. The colour designation refers to the particular experience of an individual in certain situations, which is independent from the given spectral composition of light. Against this background, the phenomena of illusory colours can be explained. In brief, the objective of my research was then to compare the activity of the nervous system with the activity of the nervous system, and to conceive of the nervous system as a closed system.

Poerksen: Comparing this experiment on the colour perception of pigeons with the striking behaviour of the manipulated salamanders, we find ourselves facing the same situation: the focus is always on internal states, not on their purported external determinants — coloured objects or moving worms.

Maturana: Yes — and suddenly I was forced to consider what "knowing" actually meant if the experiments were to be taken seriously. It is no longer possible to refer to external objects that determine what we perceive. What does it mean "to know" if we consider the nervous system as a closed system?

Poerksen: If I understand correctly, you were taught by your experiments. But this is the classical procedure of the realists: they propose a hypothesis, test it, it fails — and they modify it. The circumstances, the real world, force them to revise their ideas. The course and the direction of your thinking, are they not essentially realistic?

Maturana: This is an interesting point. We might, of course, say that I acted like a realist when I changed the traditional problems of the theory of knowledge in such a way as to be led to reject realism. But that is not of primary importance. I would claim that a scientist, and not a philosopher, was at work there, who tackled the problem of the possible existence and the degree of influence of an external reality. The distinction between science and philosophy that I am suggesting here has to do with the question of what philosophers and scientists want to preserve and sustain when they develop a theory. Their intentions are different. Philosophical theories arise, I would claim, when we try to preserve certain explanatory principles that we consider valid a priori. This interest in the preservation of principles and their coherence justifies disregarding what may be experienced. Scientific theories, on the contrary, arise when we want to preserve the coherences in relation to what we are capable of experiencing. The scientist can, therefore, ignore principles — dissolve them — and design a scientific theory. That is precisely what I did. I started out from the coherences within experience, I investigated the colour perception of pigeons, i.e., I investigated the operations of living systems — and had to do terrible things to them for the purposes of my research. The question as to whether an external reality really existed had little relevance for me; it was not one of my problems.

The limits of external determination

Poerksen: Can you see experiments and experiences that might refute your present claims and put you back on the path of realism?

Maturana: I could only give up my views if the structural determinism of living systems were no longer in force. What happens in any living system, we must bear in mind, is necessarily determined by its structure and not specifiable by external influences. However, the assumption that living systems are structure-determined systems is in no way related to an observer-independent reality; it is an abstraction resulting from the coherences that observers may experience.

Poerksen: What do you mean by *structural determinism*?

Maturana: When you press the key of your recording machine with your index finger in order to record our conversation, then you expect the machine to record. Should the machine fail to do so, you would certainly not go and see a doctor to have the functioning of your index finger checked. You will take the recording machine to someone who understands its structure and will, therefore, be able to repair it so that it will react to the pressure of your index finger in the appropriate way. This means that we treat your little recording machine as a system in which everything that happens in it or to it, is determined by its structure. My claim is that this structural determinism is valid for all systems. Human beings are structure-determined systems, too.

Poerksen: In what ways? Could you give another example?

Maturana: Suppose you see a doctor about a pain in your stomach. You will be properly examined — and perhaps your appendix will be removed. So you will be treated like a structure-determined system: the pain you felt before the operation and the relief you experienced afterwards were both determined by your structure and its modification by the doctor. More generally, this means that an external agent impinging on some molecular system triggers certain effects but cannot determine them. Any impingement from outside merely triggers some structural dynamics; all its consequences are, however, specified and determined by the structure of the system itself.

Poerksen: Is this so? Let us assume I offer you medicinal tablets or hard drugs and we both take some; we shall experience similar things. Drugs have quite specific effects.

Maturana: Perfectly correct, but the similarity of our experiences does not refute structural determinism at all. Taking drugs means bringing molecules with a specific structure into your organism, which then become part of it and modify the structure of its nervous system. What happens will, however, necessarily depend on the structure of the nervous system itself. Without receptors inside the organism for the substances you put in, nothing can happen at all. A receptor, one must remember, is a specific molecular configuration that matches the structure of the substance in question, a drug, for instance. In this way, a change in the organism is triggered.

Poerksen: Does this mean that the thesis of the structural determinism of all systems is essentially irrefutable? In other words, can you state conditions under which something dead or alive would no longer be subject to universal structural determinism?

Maturana: Only a miracle can violate structural determinism and make it inoperative. Suddenly the impossible seems possible. Even observing then appears to be something wonderful and miraculous — and is therefore inexplicable.

Poerksen: Are you waiting for a miracle?

Maturana: No, I do not expect a miracle. And, quite generally, I do not think that we could really do very much with miracles.

Poerksen; Why not? Miracles, to me, are glorious moments in which something suddenly loses its traditional validity.

Maturana: On the contrary. Miracles are rather impractical events. Just remember the story of King Midas of Phrygia who offered his services to the god Dionysos. It shows — in a satirical way for me — the uselessness of miracles that suspend structural determinism. Dionysos asked King Midas what kind of reward he wanted for his services. King Midas answered that he wanted everything he touched to turn into gold. And that is what it happened. He touched the grass — it became gold; he touched the table — gold! Happily, he went home, and his daughter came running towards him; he embraced her — and she became rigid and turned into a golden statue. What is the tragedy of King Midas? My answer: His tragedy was that he had no chance of becoming an analytical chemist. Everything he touched was the same for him: gold.

The powerlessness of power

Poerksen: You claim that human beings are structure-determined systems, too. This conception sets narrow limits for the concept of direct and linear control. However, is not the wielding of power and force by dictators a compelling example of how extensively people can be controlled and influenced by external forces, after all?

Maturana: No, that is not the case. As I have lived under a dictatorial regime, I know what I am talking about. Strangely enough, power arises only when there is obedience. It is the consequence of an act of submission depending on the decisions and the structure of the individuals subjecting themselves. It is granted to dictators by doing what they want. You grant power to others in order to keep or save something — life, freedom, possessions, jobs, a relationship, etc. My thesis is, in brief: *Power arises through submission.* When dictators or other people point a gun at me and want to force me to do something, then I am the one who has to consider: Do I want to grant power to these people? Perhaps it is sensible to meet their demands for some time in order to be able to get the better of them in favourable circumstances.

Poerksen: Does what you are saying also apply to the dictatorship of the National Socialists? Was it the terror of the Gestapo that made Adolf Hitler powerful? Or did the people actually decide to grant power to a third-class painter from Austria?

Maturana: It was a conscious or a subconscious decision of the people, which gave power to Adolf Hitler. All those who did not protest had decided not to protest. They had decided to subject themselves. Suppose a dictator comes along and kills every person refusing to obey him. Suppose the people of the country refuse to obey him. The consequence: He kills and kills. But for how long? Well, in the extreme case he will go on killing until everybody is dead. Where is the dictator's power then? It has vanished.

Poerksen: How do you want us to interpret this re-formulation of the relationship between power and helplessness? Is this an idealistic call not to subject ourselves? Or do you really mean what you are saying?

Maturana: I am totally serious when I say: we always do what we want to do, even though we may claim to be acting against our will or to have been compelled to do something. Nobody can force you to shoot at another person but you may, of course, decide to shoot in order to save your own life. Maintaining that you were forced to shoot is only an excuse that obscures the goal you were pursuing, namely, to save your life for the price of subjecting yourself. When you decide, in such a situation, not to shoot at another person, a shot may still be heard but it will be a shot fired at you — and you might die, preserving your dignity.

Poerksen: The Chilean dictator Pinochet ordered, as we all know, the abduction, torture and murder of many of his opponents. How did you experience this phase of Chilean history? What did you do when Salvador Allende was dead and the socialist experiment had met with a bloody end?

Maturana: I decided to practise hypocrisy in order to stay alive and to protect my family and children. At the same time, I tried to move and behave in such a way as to avoid endangering my dignity and my self-respect. I kept away from certain situations, respected the curfew, did not discuss certain topics in the university. When the soldiers came and ordered me to raise my hands and to move up to the wall, I raised my hands and moved up to the wall. However, it was quite clear to me in those moments that the time would come when I would no longer be prepared to grant power to the dictator's regime.

Poerksen: Would you like to tell me about a particular situation?

Maturana: One day in the year 1977 I was arrested and put into prison. The reason was that I had given three lectures. The first lecture dealt with Genesis and the Fall. I said that Eve who had eaten from the apple and then given it to Adam could serve as an example. She was disobedient, and her rebellion against the divine commandment laid the foundation for human self-knowledge and responsible action, for the expulsion from paradise, a world without self-knowledge. In the second lecture, I spoke about St. Francis of Assisi. His way of perceiving human beings, in my eyes, generates such deep respect towards them that it becomes impossible to define them as enemies. And I added that every army must first transform other human beings into strangers and then into enemies in order to be able to maltreat and kill them. The third lecture was devoted to Jesus and the New Testament. How do we live together, I asked my audience, if we base everything on the emotion of love? A few days later, I was taken to prison and treated like a prisoner. I was to be interrogated, I heard. One day somebody arrived and called out my name and said: "Are you Professor Humberto Maturana?" When I heard that I thought that I would remain a professor forever even if these people killed me. The status of professor was the protective shield they had granted me. They took me to a room where three persons were waiting. I sat down and asked the question: "In what way have I violated the statement of principles issued by the military government?" This means that it was me who began the interrogation and changed the rules of the game. I would not say that I manipulated those people but that the interrogation took place in a way that allowed me to keep my dignity and self-respect. I continued behaving like a professor and tried to counter the accusations they formulated. And I gave these people a lecture on evolutionary theory and explained to them why they would never be able to destroy communism by persecuting communists. I said that it was necessary to change or eliminate the conditions that made communism possible, in the first place. The three men listened to me with growing astonishment. I told them they could invite me for a lecture any time. Then they took me back to the university.

Poerksen: Your very own experiences during the years of the dictatorship are most important to me because they make me understand you better, I believe. You do not plead for some fatal heroism, you do not condemn those who subject themselves, but you plead for a maximum of awareness in the handling of power.

Maturana: Naturally, yes. It can be very stupid not to subject oneself for a time and to wait for a suitable opportunity to strike back. My fundamental point is to declare one's responsibility and to invite others to act in full awareness. Does one want the world that emerges when one grants power to others? Does one primarily want to survive? Does one reject the world emerging through the wielding of power in an unconditional and uncompromising way?

Poerksen: Do you believe that that different state of awareness is really decisive? It might be argued that conscious or subconscious subjection leads to the same consequences: the dictator stays in power.

Maturana: This different state of awareness is decisive because it allows you to be hypocritical. Being hypocritical means simulating a non-existent emotion. You remain an observer, keeping an inner distance, and one day you may act

in a different way again. This means that the perceptual abili-
ties of the hypocrites are not destroyed, and their self-respect
and dignity are preserved. Due to these decisive and very significant experiences, they may be able to lead a different life. If
one gives up this attitude of the conscious handling of power,
one is lost because one has decided for blindness.

Poerksen: How can we be sure that the belief that we are
merely hypocritical and observing is not just a subtle and
refined form of self-delusion?

Maturana: Well, that is a difficult problem, indeed. The situation is particularly precarious when people are convinced that
they are immune to the temptations of power. These people
have become blind to their own temptability, to the delights of
wielding power, the pleasures of the uncontrolled execution
of control. My view is that we should never believe that we are
in any way special as far as morality or anything else is concerned: we are then mentally unprepared for situations that
may make torturers of us. Those who think they are immune
will be the first, I believe, to become torturers in certain situations. They are not aware of their own seducibility. Whatever
horrible or wonderful things one human being can do – there
will always be another, and it could be you or me, who is capable of doing the same. Such an insight allows us to lead our
lives in full awareness and to decide whether to support
democracy or a dictatorship.

The emergence of blind spots

Poerksen: At the end of 1973 — following the coup of the military under Pinochet — many members of the university fled to
other countries. You remained. Why?

Maturana: On the day of the military coup I rang my friend
Heinz von Foerster and asked him to help me and my family to
leave the country. Heinz von Foerster tried to get me an invitation from an American university, which was not at all easy, of
course. Nobody wanted me. Ten days later, Heinz von
Foerster had managed to interest a neurophysiologist in New
York in my work. But by that time I had already decided to
stay in Chile. My motives to stay were of different kinds. My
first thought was: If all democratically minded people left the
country there would soon be no recollection of a democratic

culture and of another, a better time. In this perspective, every older person was a living treasure. Then I was concerned about the fate of all the many students who were dispirited and suddenly found themselves drifting through the university on their own. Many professors had fled or gone into hiding, or had already been arrested. Finally, I wanted to know what it means to live under a dictator. I wanted to understand the Germans and, in particular, the history of my friend Heinz von Foerster who had survived the Nazi terror due to his understanding of systems. He once said to me: The more specified a system is the easier it is to cheat. I also asked myself whether I might be able to observe in such a dictatorial system how people gradually go blind, and what the causes of such perceptual deprivation were. Can one, if one has been duly forewarned and is aware of the dangers of ideologically produced blindness, prevent it from developing and retain one's capabilities of vision and perception?

Poerksen: You wanted to come to grips with the epistemology of ideologies.

Maturana: You might put it that way, yes. When innumerable Germans insisted after the War that they had known nothing about the horrors of the Nazi period, I was convinced that not all of them were liars. Perhaps some of them were simply unable to face up to the terrible truth. I wanted to know what had been going on inside them and in their psyches. How does one live under a dictatorial regime that makes it so very difficult to keep away from it? In what measure does one unavoidably go blind even though one definitely does not want it to happen? Does one go blind because one knows that one could? How and in what ways is blindness produced at all?

Poerksen: What did you observe?

Maturana: Nobody is everywhere. If you decree curfews, you prevent people from seeing certain things. They will be unable to notice that people are murdered in their street during the night; they will not see the corpses. Everything happens behind a curtain. So people might not believe the rumours and tales they come across when they go out in the morning. There is nothing to be seen, not even a trace of blood. Moreover, people will probably say to themselves that soldiers are human beings too, and that no human being can behave in such bestial ways. Such humanist presumptions may therefore very well make us blind: they protect us against the horror and they preserve our trust in other people. Of course, the new situation of a dictatorship creates new advantages for some people: Suddenly particular jobs are available because other people had to give them up and get away.

Poerksen: I find it striking that you and various other authors, who are counted among the founders of constructivism today, all had to suffer under dictatorial regimes and were confronted with dogmatic worldviews. Heinz von Foerster had to hide from the NS-thugs; Ernst von Glasersfeld left Vienna when the Nazis seized power; Paul Watzlawick has repeatedly suggested how deeply shocked he was by the NS-regime; Francisco Varela escaped from Pinochet to Costa Rica. And so on. Is there a connection between the theories of these authors and the experience of dictatorship? Alternatively, is this biographical correspondence purely accidental?

Maturana: It is not accidental but the result of the period. Infinitely many people were confronted with authoritarian systems more or less directly during the past century — the century of the Russian Revolution, of Fascism and National Socialism. I can, of course, only speak for myself, but my own understanding of power does not derive from the experiences I went through after the military coup in Chile. Rather the reverse. My life under the dictatorship was informed by my understanding of power, resulting from my permanent longing for democracy. Supporting democracy obviously entails the rejection of dictatorship that, therefore, becomes an enemy and a constant threat lurking in the background. All those actively engaged in the democratisation of a country quickly realise how difficult and laborious it is to keep a democratic culture alive. One has to come to terms with the ideal of perfection, which is widespread and deep-rooted in our culture, and with the attempt to generate seemingly perfect and allegedly democratic forms of living together even with the means of oppression. One is evidently opposed to dictatorship and, consequently, an active supporter of the individual, not of the goals of some collective. Still, one must not lose sight of the whole of society when working for the democratic participation of the individual. The persons you mentioned have, I think, been well aware of these difficulties and understood that there is no antagonism between individual and society. This is what they all have in common.

Poerksen: Structure-determined systems — human beings — can only be controlled in a limited way; one can perturb them but not control them. My thesis is: You have developed an epistemology that removes the conceptual foundation of dictatorial power.

Maturana: I strongly support this thesis and want to add that I destroy the conceptual foundations of dictatorship because my work allows me to achieve a more profound understanding of democracy. Democracy must be created anew every day, I believe, as a space of living together in which participation and cooperation are possible, based on self-respect and the respect of others. The first thing a dictatorship destroys is the self-respect and the autonomy of every single individual, because it demands subjection and obedience as the price for staying alive.

Poerksen: Could it be that the immense popularity of your ideas today is due to the often-invoked end of all ideologies and the collapse of the sort of socialism that "really existed"?

Maturana: I see a connection. What I have written provides a new foundation for the possibility of self-respect, which is fundamentally negated by dictatorships. What the readers of my work may realise is that we are all unavoidably participating in the creation of the world we live in. We bring forth the world that we live. This is the view that I invite people to try without compulsion or cost, a view that values the individual. And whoever feels appreciated and respected, will be enabled to appreciate and respect themselves. They can accept the responsibility for what they do. It is indeed as the Beatles song proclaims: *All you need is love.* We are all looking for love, and still cannot help being scared of it. And now, to make matters worse, a scientist stands up and starts talking about love! Some of the people reading these passages may think that he must be mad! Nevertheless, it is a fact that all we want is love. And what is love? Love means to live in a community that is supported by self-respect and mutual respect and cooperation.

Language and self-observation

Poerksen: Does the idea of responsibility for this self-generated and perhaps love-influenced world not fly in the face of structural determinism? Can structure-determined systems be held responsible for anything? A dog that attacks me because it feels threatened is evidently a structure-determined system. However, we would never think of ascribing responsibility to it or condemning it because we do not consider it an autonomous being capable of free decision. Therefore, freedom is the prerequisite of responsibility. If you, however, describe human beings generally as structure-determined systems, then you necessarily negate, I would assert, the possibility of responsibility.

Maturana: Perfectly correct. Living systems cannot act responsibly because they know no purpose or goal; they simply live in the flow of existence. Only human beings can assume responsibility in the domain of relations because they exist in language. They are capable of describing a certain action as responsible. Language enables us to reflect and distinguish the consequences of our actions for other living beings and to classify them as responsible or irresponsible. In this way, our caring for other people gains presence – and the possibility of responsible action arises.

Poerksen: But, surely, this requires freedom. Any person desiring to act ethically must have the freedom of choice and self-determined decision. Repeating the question: Do not your key concepts of structural determinism and your special understanding of autonomy force you to abandon the idea of freedom and, consequently, the possibility of responsible action?

Maturana: The experience of choice and decision, which we human beings make, does not at all contradict our structure-determinedness. Human beings will always remain structure-determined systems; they may, however, by virtue of a perspective opening up in a meta-domain, make the experience that they have a choice. Then they move in another domain but still operate as structure-determined systems. This experience of the potential choice between different possibilities, however, is a unique characteristic of the human species and requires language. Having a choice presupposes the ability to observe and compare at least two different situations appearing at the same time, and then to adapt one's perspective in such a way as to be able to make out a difference between these situations. At first one sees only sameness and is blocked. A change of perspective and position may enable us to see potential distinctions in what appears to be the same; then we can move – according to our own preferences and ways of life – and choose one possibility while negating others. As this process is an intentional act in the language of living beings, it is possible to classify it, from the point of view of an observer, as a process of choice.

Poerksen: Does this mean that it is the meta-perspective that makes it possible to identify an action as an act of choice and decision?

Maturana: Exactly so, yes. Only from that perspective does it become possible to characterise something as a choice and a decision between different possibilities. We perform an operation on a meta-level because we have the ability to use language and to make ourselves aware of an event and its consequences. In this act of becoming aware, the phenomena we are dealing with are transformed into objects of contemplation. We gain a form of distance that we lack when we are completely immersed in our activities and situations. If we accept this and consider it adequate, an action may then be described as *responsible* or as *irresponsible*.

Poerksen: Could you elucidate these ideas by means of a particular case?

Maturana: Some time ago, reports travelled round the world that a boy who had been trying to get to Miami together with his mother in a small boat from Cuba was saved from drowning by dolphins. For some reason, their boat sank and the mother drowned. The boy, however, was kept afloat by a school of dolphins, saved from drowning, and finally rescued. What those dolphins did we can, as beings living in language, describe as *responsible*. The dolphins do not, as far as we know, possess the ability to comment on their activities and to tell us about what happened between them and the boy floating on the sea. However, *we* are capable of talking about the relationship between those animals and the boy because we operate in the domain of language. We can characterise what happened as an effort to keep another being alive. From this meta-perspective the activity of the dolphins appears as a responsible action.

Poerksen: To act responsibly, then, means to take care of someone else and then to observe one's actions and classify them accordingly.

Maturana: Exactly. People are aware of the circumstances and reflect the consequences of their activities. They can ask themselves whether they want to be what they are as they are doing what they are doing. In the moment of self-observation, all the certainties and securities of the state without reflection disappear. When, through the linguistic operation, a form of contemplation and an awareness has been generated that allows observation, then people will, at the next step, act according to their own preferences, that means they will act responsibly. And when they, with a further step, try to find out whether they value their own preferences and intend to maintain them, then they are free. Do I like my predilections? Do I like the decision I have taken and of which I have just said that I like it and that it corresponds with my desires? In this moment of the reflection of their own choice, there arises the experience of freedom.

Poerksen: I want to keep on questioning: How can a structure-determined system feel responsible for its own actions? If I cannot control and influence others then the effects of my activities become completely incalculable. We are confronted by a *paradox of responsibility* because we are to be held responsible for something the consequences of which we could not possibly foresee. Doing good may potentially trigger terrible consequences (and *vice versa*).

Maturana: The concept of responsibility is ambiguous. Some authors mean by responsibility that we must be accountable for all the possible consequences of an action. Responsibility then means causation. For me, responsible action is a question of awareness. Persons act or fail to act in the awareness of all the possible and desirable consequences of their actions. It is not necessary for the consequences of an action to be fully calculable and foreseeable; there may indeed be undesirable consequences in the end. In my view, being responsible simply means to be in a certain state of attention and mindfulness:

one's activities match one's desires in a reflected way, that is all.

Poerksen: The concept of responsibility is, for you, not linked to the idea that it is possible to plan the consequences of an action?

Maturana: This is not relevant. To plan something means to envisage ways and procedures for achieving a certain result and to subordinate the next chosen steps to this imagined result. The potential consequences of an action need not come about, however, and perhaps they exist only in the minds of particular people. It is crucial, in any case, that the people designing things in this way live responsibly and act in full awareness of the possible consequences of their actions. They are responsible for what they say and do. Nevertheless, they are not accountable for what other people make of what they say and do.

Are social systems autopoietic?

Poerksen: Professor Maturana, the concepts you have created now circulate in the scientific community all over the world. However, during the three days we have been talking to each other here, you have not even once used the concept that has become a trendy designer term in the scientific community: autopoiesis. Why? Is there a deeper reason for this abstinence?

Maturana: The reason simply is that I use the concept only when it is adequate and necessary. *Autopoiesis* means "self-creation" and consists of the Greek words *autos* (self) and *poiein* (produce, create). The concept of autopoiesis supplies the answer to the question what characterizes a living system. In the course of the history of biology it has been claimed that living beings are characterised by the capability of reproduction and mobility, by a specific chemical composition, a specific aspect of metabolism, or by some combination of these different criteria. I propose another criterion. When you regard a living system you always find a network of processes or molecules that interact in such a way as to produce molecules that through their interactions in turn produce the very network that produced them and determine its boundary. Such a network I call autopoietic. Whenever you encounter a network whose operations eventually produce itself as a result, you are facing an autopoietic system. It produces itself. This system is open to the input of matter but closed with regard to the dynamics of the relations that generate it. In brief, I use the concept of autopoiesis in order to describe the key property of living beings. That is all. Whenever people are not dealing with this problem but with other topics, I do not see any reason why the concept of autopoiesis should be used.

Poerksen: Perhaps an example demonstrating the autopoiesis of the living would be helpful at this stage. You have often referred to the cell as an autopoietic system. Would that be a compelling model?

Maturana: In my terminology the cell is described as a molecular autopoietic system of the first order. This means that a cell as a totality is an autopoietic system in its own right. Consequently, multicellular organisms are autopoietic systems of the second order that are related to other organisms in diverse social, parasitic, symbiotic, and other ways. We must, quite fundamentally, realise that living systems form totalities and represent independent entities, and that there must be boundaries and edges that constitute the difference between a system and its environment. The special thing about cellular metabolism is that it produces components, which are integrated as entireties into the network of transformations that produced them. The production of components embodies, therefore, the condition of the possibility of an edge, of a boundary, of the membrane of a cell. This membrane, in turn, participates in the ongoing processes of transformation, it participates in the autopoietic dynamics of the cell: it is in itself the condition of the possibility of the operation of a network of transformations that produces the network as an integral whole. Without the boundary of the cell membrane everything would dissolve into some sort of molecular slime, and the molecules would diffuse in all directions. There would no longer be an independent entity.

Poerksen: This means that the cell produces the membrane and the membrane the cell. The producer, the act of production, and the product, have become indistinguishable.

Maturana: I would say, a little more rigorously: The molecules of the cell membrane participate in the realisation of the autopoietic processes of the cell and in the production of other molecules within the autopoietic network of the cell; and autopoiesis generates the molecules of the membrane. They produce each other, and they participate in the constitution of the whole.

Poerksen: You have been trying hard to retain the rigorous concept of autopoiesis exclusively for the characterisation of the living. Nevertheless, your readers and devotees are not willing to follow you. On the contrary: your ideas are now commonly used in social theory, in the description of society. Meanwhile, everything is an autopoietic system – science, journalism, football, families, art, politics, societies, etc. –, everything vibrates along according to its own rules within its own boundaries.

Maturana: That is so. People like and honour me as the inventor of the term and the concept of autopoiesis – particularly so, when I am not present and unable to tell them what I really said. When I appear in person, however, I always point out that the concept is, in my opinion, only valid for a certain defined domain for which it solves a particular problem. A few years ago, for instance, I was invited to a conference at the London School of Economics, which dealt with the problem of whether social systems could be seen as autopoietic. The debate lasted three full days and, at the end, I was asked to say a few concluding words. I said: "For three days I have been listening to your ideas and exchanges, and I want to put the following question to you now: What are the features of a social system that would justify choosing as the topic of this conference the problem whether a social system could be classified as autopoietic or not?"

Poerksen: You meant to suggest a different starting point for their deliberations: one must first understand the social phenomena before one can attempt to describe them more precisely with a concept borrowed from biology.

Maturana: Precisely. Applying the concept of autopoiesis to explain social phenomena will cause them to vanish from your field of vision because your whole attention will be absorbed by the concept of autopoiesis. Naturally, we can discuss whether the house we are sitting in now is an autopoietic system. The choice of this topic, however, has the unavoidable effect that the features of an autopoietic system will guide our reflections. Asking for the constitutive properties of the entity of a house, however, and whether its characteristics accord with the concept of autopoiesis, will leave us free to analyse and investigate. We might then find that houses cannot be described as autopoietic — or must be described as such. Who knows?

Poerksen: In Germany, the sociologist Niklas Luhmann at Bielefeld University has been one of the best-known proponents of the theory of autopoiesis. He introduced the concept in his central work *Soziale Systeme*, published in 1984, and from there went on to elaborate this theory by describing all the different domains of society as self-directed producers of their own specific realities. Luhmann brought about the *autopoietic turn* in sociology.

Maturana: When I was a visiting professor at Bielefeld I never withheld my criticism but articulated it frequently in numerous debates. "Thank you for having made me famous in Germany," I said to Niklas Luhmann, "but I disagree with the way in which you are using my ideas. I suggest that we start with the question of the characteristics of social phenomena. The concept of society historically precedes the idea of the autopoiesis of living systems. Society was the primary subject of debate; autopoiesis and social systems came much later. It follows, therefore, that we should first deal with all the relevant phenomena appearing in the analyses of society and only afterwards ask ourselves whether they may be elucidated more precisely in terms of the concept of autopoiesis."

Poerksen: You are cautioning against the dangers of reductionism.

Maturana: The problem simply is that Niklas Luhmann uses the concept of autopoiesis as a principle in the explanation of social phenomena, which does not illuminate the processes to be described nor the social phenomena but tends to obscure them. Autopoiesis as a biological phenomenon involves a network of molecules that produces molecules. Molecules produce molecules, form themselves into other molecules, and may be divided into molecules. Niklas Luhmann, however, does not proceed from molecules producing molecules; for him everything revolves around communications producing communications. He believes that the phenomena are similar and that the situations are comparable. That is incorrect because molecules produce molecules without extraneous help, without support. This means: autopoiesis takes place in a domain in which the interactions of the elements constituting it bring forth elements of the same kind; that is crucial. Communications, however, presuppose human beings that communicate. Communications can only produce communications with the help of human beings. The decision to replace molecules by communications places communications at the centre and excludes the human beings actually communicating. The human beings are excluded and even considered irrelevant; they only serve as the background and the basis into which the social system — conceived of as an autopoietic network of communications — is embedded.

Poerksen: What swims into focus if we follow this perspective and describe a social system as a network of autopoietically self-reproducing communications, is an extremely weird social structure: a society without human beings.

Maturana: That is precisely the form of description manufactured by Niklas Luhmann. His conception can be compared with a statistical view of social systems: people with particular features do not feature in it. When we speak about social systems in our everyday life, however, we naturally have in mind all the individuals with their peculiar properties, who would protest against their characterisation as autopoietic networks — and do so, anyway, when they criticise Niklas Luhmann. But why does he proceed in this way? He told me once that he excluded human beings from his theoretical framework in order to be able to make universal statements. If you speak about human individuals, he argued, you cannot formulate universal statements. I do not share this view, either.

Poerksen: The systems theory designed by Niklas Luhmann could perhaps be considered as a sort of *negative anthropology*: We cannot but remain silent in gentle humility and reverence regarding the infinitely manifold and ineffable mystery of humanity, the object of worship.

Maturana: That is possible; but even in the face of such a proposal you will have to take account of the people who may possibly complain and protest against their characterisation. If you deprive people of this opportunity, you treat them like freely disposable objects; they have the status of slaves, compelled to function without the opportunity of complaining when they do not like what is happening to them. Such treatment and contempt of people is standard practice in certain companies, communities, and countries that negate individuals. A social system that forbids and even fundamentally excludes complaint and protest is not a social system. It is a system of tyranny.

The dutiful worship of systems

Poerksen: The concept of autopoiesis has created a furore not only in science and amongst the followers of Niklas Luhmann but also won huge popularity in the New-Age scene. I think we are witnessing a sort of paradigm change with the theorists and opinion leaders of the New Age. Years ago they were attracted by modern physics and the dance of the atoms. It used to be reported that the physicist Werner Heisenberg, the creator of the Uncertainty Principle, and the Buddha, practically shared an identical view of the essence of matter. The syncretism that emerged could be called *quantum theology*. For some time now, the key concepts of the New-Age scene have been provided by Gregory Bateson, Francisco Varela and — Humberto Maturana. The protagonists of the scene — Capra & Co. — have been brewing a rather explosive mixture of spiritualism and science, a sort of *network theology*, which is supposed to be the scientifically legitimated foundation of the worship of universal connectedness.

Maturana: We have now hit upon the problem of reductionism, which is characteristic of our culture. Just look out the window for a moment. Over there, you see a loving couple, a young woman and a young man kissing each other. What is happening there? My answer would be: Whatever happens there happens in the domain of human relations.

Naturally, you can point out that in such exchanges of tenderness hormones and neurotransmitters are involved; no doubt we can speak of systemic processes in both organisms. All that would be correct, but what is occurring in the encounter of those two persons, their feeling of love, is not grasped or described by reference to such processes: the loving tender relation that those two persons are living cannot be reduced to hormones, neurotransmitters and systemic processes. What they are actively living occurs in them in the flow of their inter-actions as these give rise to the flow of what they do with each other through them. When Fritjof Capra and others promote their quantum theology or some network theology and begin to worship systems or networks, they are thinking and argu-ing in a reductionist way. They flatten and blur everything. They no longer speak of molecules but only of systems that they elevate to their new gods. This is obviously reductionism, too. What I do is fundamentally different from a reductionist approach. Since I am always aware of the existence of different non-intersecting phenomenal domains, I take care not to con-fuse them in my thinking or in my writing. Indeed, if one does this, one can see that the phenomena of one domain cannot be expressed in terms of the phenomena of another domain.

Thus, whatever happens in the domain of the operation of the organism as a totality in its relational space cannot be expressed in terms of the molecules that compose it, or vice versa. All that an observer can do is to see what happens in those two domains and attempt to establish a generative rela-tion between them. I preserve, and attend to, the differences between the separate phenomenal domains in my descrip-tions. In this way, one sees the domain of molecules, the sys-temic domain, the domain of relations, etc. All these different domains constitute their own specific phenomena.

Poerksen: Although I am not particularly inclined to defend the New-Age scene against anything, I think that it is no acci-dent that your work has become attractive to that scene. The thesis of the observer-dependence of all knowledge can be interpreted as the removal of the subject-object rift that we encounter in the description of spiritual and mystical experi-ences.

Maturana: These spiritual experiences have, in my opinion, nothing to do with experiences of transcendence in an ontolog-ical sense but much rather with an extension of awareness and an intensified feeling of participation: You become aware of being all at one with other human beings, with the cosmos, the biosphere, etc. When people now talk about spiritual matters, however, they generally refer to some experience containing an ontological understanding or a true knowledge of nature. Such insights are, in my view, impossible in principle. Noth-ing that can be said is independent from us.

Poerksen: Have you yourself had experiences that might be described as spiritual in your sense?

Maturana: I suffered from lung tuberculosis as a young man. After having spent seven months in bed, I went back to my school to find out whether I could still complete the school year in the regular way and so avoid having to repeat it. It was in December and I — having just got out of my sickbed — had to listen to a presentation prepared by my fellow pupils concerning the menace of tuberculosis. They described the terrible risks of this disease and the extremely limited opportunities for therapy available at the time. While I was listening to them, I felt myself slowly beginning to faint and decided to observe this process of fainting. When I regained consciousness, I was in the middle of the room and heard the voice of my teacher who said that I was looking very green and wanted to know what had happened.

Poerksen: What had happened?

Maturana: I shall tell you how I experienced the situation. When I prepared to observe the process of passing out, I lost all feeling for my body. I had no body any more but was still aware of being alive and gradually disappearing — like a wisp of smoke floating quietly and silently through a room — in a glorious blue cosmos. I felt like dissolving into that magnificent blue, fusing, and becoming one with everything. Then suddenly everything was over. My head ached, I was sick; I heard the voice of my teacher and came round. What does this wonderful experience mean, I asked myself. Had I seen God? Was it a mystical experience? Or had I been on the way to death? In the following weeks and months, I read the few books that existed at the time about near-death experiences and studied the medical and the mystical literature. It became obvious to me that I walked a very thin line with all the different interpretations. Reading the medical books and accepting their statements led me to believe that I had experienced what it is like to die and what effects are caused by insufficient blood supply to the brain. If I believed the mystical literature, my experience involved an encounter with God and the unification with the totality of existence. At the time, I opted for the medical interpretation of what had happened to me as a near-death experience.

Poerksen: Are these two interpretations so very different? Death could be a metaphor telling us of the gift of a new beginning: the old personality is dying.

Maturana: It was, in any case, an experience that transformed my life. This transformation and the element of the extension of awareness restored to my experience a spiritual, a mystical, dimension that was not so clear to me when I was young and thought I had to decide between the two interpretations. I lost all fear of death; I stopped clinging to things and unreasonably identifying myself with them because through the encounter with death I had experienced my connectedness with the whole. I became more reflective and less dogmatic. This is not intended to mean that I want to describe myself as an illuminated being above all earthly ties, not at all. That experience was so penetrating that it changed my life. Everything is transient, I realised, nothing but transition. We do not have to defend anything, we cannot hold on to anything.

CHAPTER 4

Truth is what works

Francisco J. Varela on cognitive science,
Buddhism, the inseparability of subject and object,
and the exaggerations of constructivism

Francisco J. Varela (1946–2001) studied biology in Santiago de Chile, obtained his doctorate 1970 at Harvard University with a thesis on the insect eye, and worked there for some time in the laboratory of Torsten Wiesel, the later Nobel Laureate for medicine. From his scientific beginnings as a researcher in biology, he did not only study and practise biology but, resisting the dominating mainstream, pursued a research programme that ignored and broke down traditional disciplinary boundaries. This research programme is best characterised as *experimental epistemology,* a concept introduced by the neuropsychiatrist and cybernetician Warren S. McCulloch. Varela's great aspiration was to examine and answer the philosophical ur-question of cognition with scientific precision and with the help of the best possible theoretical framework.

Having obtained his doctorate, he went back to Chile to work as a professor of biology together with Humberto R. Maturana. He contributed to the writing of the theory of autopoiesis which was to cause a furore in the world of science as a universally applicable explanatory model. After the overthrow of Allende and the installation of the dictatorship by the putsch general Pinochet, Varela first escaped to Costa Rica, then became professor at the American universities of Colorado and New York, and finally returned in 1980 to the

University of Chile in Santiago for five years. Temporary positions as guest professor for neurobiology, philosophy, and cognitive science in Germany, Switzerland and France led him to Paris, in the end, where he worked as a research director of the Centre National de Recherche Scientifique until his death on 28 May 2001.

In his research work embracing cognitive science, evolutionary theory, and immunology, Varela, constantly inspired by his fundamental interest in the key questions of epistemology, gave the epistemological debate a new orientation. In his thinking, he refuses to accept the strict separation of subject and object, of knower and known, which as a rule unites realists and constructivists alike. Varela rejects the fundamental dualism dividing mind and world, which had shaped Western philosophy from its earliest beginnings. He does not subscribe to the idea that human individuals can invent their own realities blindly and arbitrarily, and without experiencing any resistance from the external world and all other things given. He equally distances himself, however, from the diametrically opposite position that overstates the inherent power of the world of objects. The external world and all other things given cannot determine what happens in an organism. Francisco J. Varela's claim is that individual and world create each other.

The computational model of the mind

Poerksen: The ancient key questions of philosophy are at the centre of modern cognitive science. What is the essence of the mind? Do our conceptions represent a given world, which is independent from our minds? What is the formative power of external objects over our perceptions? How does cognition function? The search for an adequate answer and an improved understanding of the human mind has led many cognitive scientists to entertain the assumption that the brain is actually a kind of computer. Memory is taken to be a store. Thinking and perceiving are understood as data processing in the sense that an independent external world is computationally transformed into symbols and represented in the organism in this manner. You are very critical of this view. Why?

Varela: If the brain is considered as a kind of computer then cognitive research is limited to discovering certain self-sufficient shapes — the symbols — together with the rules governing them — the programs. But this search for symbols and programs will never be profitable because it simply does not do justice to the way the brain functions. There are no symbols to be discovered in the brain; the brain is not based on software; objects or human beings are definitely not represented by way of symbols in the brain, although even most intelligent people once believed this to be so. So there is little point in searching for neuron number 25, which is supposed to represent my grandmother or some other part of the world. The brain is essentially a dynamically organised system; numerous interdependent variables have to be taken into account, which can only be dissociated from each other in an arbitrary way.

Poerksen: You are critical of the research programme based on the identification of brain and computer.

Varela: Not only that; my criticism has not only empirical but also epistemological foundations. Alone common sense finds no difficulty in understanding that living beings necessarily manifest themselves in particular actions and in their appropriate environments. The actions of an animal and the world in which it performs these actions are inseparably connected. Going through life as a small fly makes a cup of tea appear like an ocean of liquid; an elephant, however, will see the same amount of tea as an insignificant drop, tiny and barely noticeable. What is perceived appears inseparably connected with the actions and the way of life of an organism: cognition is, as I would claim, the *bringing forth of a world*, it is embodied action. Whoever, on the contrary, believes in the computer model of the mind, inevitably believes in the existence of a stable world independent from living beings. This world is recognised by living beings and represented in their nervous systems in the form of little symbols; cognition, according to this view, is a kind of computation on the basis of symbols.

Poerksen: I suppose that such a view also implies a naive kind of realism: one believes in static, given world that is represented in our cognitive apparatus.

Varela: Not necessarily. Not every cognitivist or scientist following such a model is necessarily a naive realist. The key concept rests on two central premises that admit of different epistemological interpretations. On the one hand, cognition is assumed to be essentially a form of symbol processing, which resembles the functioning of a computer. Such a conception accords with scientists of both a realist and a non-realist orientation alike. On the other hand, the relation between the cognitive system and the world is, in the classical sense, seen as a relation of semantic representation: the mind processes symbols, which represent the properties of the world in a specific way. This idea of a fundamental semantic correspondence between symbol and world is also open to interpretations that need not necessarily be realistic.

Poerksen: But surely, anyone claiming that there is some sort of correspondence between world and symbol is inevitably a realist.

Symbol and world

Varela: No, because we could say that there is a specific relation and a semantic correspondence between the word *table* and the object that we call a table. A relativist and critic of realism favouring this view would then add, for instance, that the relation between symbol and world is obviously different for an Eskimo and for a pygmy, and that they have different words, i.e. different symbols, for what we usually call a table. So even a relativist can uphold the notion of semantic correspondence.

Poerksen: Why did the computer model remain attractive for so long? It seems to me that it promised the more or less imminent explanation of brain and mind. Taking the computer as the archetype of cognition generates clearly defined research objectives, unambiguous questions, and justified hopes for success.

Varela: Exactly. I am not at all surprised by the appeal of this model because it matches common ideas and is an expression of our craving for transparency. It is deeply rooted in the rationalist traditions of the West and supported by them. The idea of representation in the form of symbols has long been the foundation of mathematics and the basis of linguistics, whereas the ideas that I pursue introduce something very novel. There is still less experience with the investigation of dynamic and emergent systems, everything becomes more complicated and less easy to penetrate. Cognition is the *bring-*

ing forth of a world; the meaning of something is no longer understood as resulting from a correspondence between an object and a symbol but as the emergence of stable impressions and patterns — invariants. These develop in the course of time. A regular pattern must have appeared first before we can take it to be a feature of a world that we consider independent from us.

Poerksen: You have published numerous studies on colour perception. How does a stable colour impression come about? How do animals or humans perceive colour?

Varela: Look here, there is a book on the table in front of us. Due to our essentially identical structure it appears in a colour that we call *green*. We human beings are the products of an evolutionary lineage along which our ancestors developed specific patterns through their encounters with the environments in which they found themselves. If we now assume that our given world and some object that we call a book have particular properties, and if we take into account the history of our descent, then these two factors yield a mutually determining invariant pattern. Both of us call this pattern a colour and name this colour *green*. But we have known for a long time now that birds, for example — due to their evolutionary history — perceive something that we simply cannot imagine: numerous birds seem to have a colour system comprising four basic colours whereas three are sufficient for us humans.

Organisms exist in different perceptual worlds, they live in different spaces of chromatic invariants. So the question arises: what does this book look like? Who is right? The birds or we? The answer is: both. These different perceptions permit both birds and humans to stay alive. The meaning of an object, its colour or its properties, emerges through long phases of coupling between organism and world. A colour is not the result of a construction taking place exclusively within the organism, nor does it exist — the other extreme — in itself and independently from the living being that perceives something. We are faced by stable qualities that can only develop on the basis of an evolutionary history. They cannot be assigned unequivocally to either the knower or the known, they cannot be clearly attributed to either the subject or the object.

Poerksen: What you call the *bringing forth of a world*, related thinkers simply designate the *construction of reality*. The difference between these two concepts is, for me, that constructivists have traditionally foregrounded the subject part. You seem to plead for a more balanced view of the relationship between subject and object. You insist: there must be both; both are indispensable for the act of cognition.

Varela: That is the central idea. Only the *co-construction* of subject and object can overcome the traditional logical geography of the strict separation of knower and known, internal and external world. There is no subject, as the constructivists suggest, on one side, constructing its reality in the desired way. And there exists no object, as the realists believe, on the other side, which determines what happens in the organism. My view is that subject and object determine and condition each other, that knower and known arise in mutual dependence, that we neither represent an external world inside nor blindly and arbitrarily construct such a world and project it outside. My plea is for a middle way that avoids both the extremes of subjectivism and idealism, and the presumptions of realism and objectivism.

The philosophical problem factory

Poerksen: Perhaps two aphorisms by Heinz von Foerster could contribute to further clarification. He epitomises the central idea of realism with the words: "The world is the cause, experience the consequence." The fundamental principle of constructivism is, however: "Experience is the cause, the world the consequence."

Varela: I do not agree with either position. As one printed version of this conversation is intended for a German audience, I should like to state quite clearly and unambiguously: I am not a realist, and I do not consider myself a constructivist, however often I may be classified as such in Germany. Classical constructivism does not at all impress me as a convincing mode of thought because it posits one side of the cognitive process as absolute: the organism forces its own logic and its own models on the world. I do not believe that to be the case at all. Such an assumption appears to me to be a relapse into neo-Kantian thinking. I have been trying for years to keep my name out of this debate — but obviously I have not been very successful.

Poerksen: To repeat the question: when confronted by the distinction between subject and object, you refuse to side with one or the other?

Varela: The goal of my work in cognitive science is not the dialectical negation of one side or the other. My question is not whether the world is represented in the organism, whether the subject is primary or whether the decisive influence is due to an object, my point is the total abolition of both extreme positions, not their affirmation or negation. My point is that neither the subject nor the object is primary. Both exist only in mutual dependence and in mutual determination.

Poerksen: If you are unable to make this decision, how can you define a clear epistemological stance?

Varela: Why do I need the decision for subject or object in order to do epistemological research, to formulate hypotheses and design research projects? The task of epistemological thought and research efforts is the question of how we can understand the way knowledge comes about and how conceptions of reality arise. The decision for subject or object already contains a definition of cognition and knowledge although that is, in fact, the problem to be solved.

Poerksen: We could argue, however, that the distinction between subject and object is the central philosophical problem factory. Those who put the object first, investigate the world — and its impingement on the subject; they practise object-centred philosophy. Those who hold the subject to be primary, analyse its peculiarities, its features, its logic. They neglect objects and practise subject-centred philosophy.

Varela: I insist: the view that an epistemologist is compelled to distinguish between subject and object in order to study the relation between the two is the heritage of Western rationalism and the Kantian theory of knowledge. This view is historically conditioned. I am sorry but I really do not want to play this game because philosophical conceptions have been available for a long time that evade this alleged coercion into dualism. The phenomenologists Edmund Husserl and Maurice

Merleau-Ponty have shown clearly that an inevitable and inseparable connection exists between what might be called a subject or an object. They are not opposites.

Poerksen: But the early studies of the phenomenologists that you incorporate in your work in cognitive science, are of a realist orientation. Edmund Husserl, the founder of phenomenology, already formulated the battle cry destined to become famous: "*Zu den Sachen selbst!*" ["To the objects themselves!"] Is that not the research programme of a realist, a turn in the direction of the object?

Varela: It is, in my opinion, one of the amusing puzzles how little Edmund Husserl, whom I value as the greatest philosopher of the 20th century, is understood in his own country, and how incredibly he is turned into a caricature of himself in German universities. What Husserl means when he speaks of the need to turn to the objects themselves, is not realism at all, definitely not. He is not concerned with something already existing in a given way. The purpose of his phenomenological work is to examine, without premature judgment, the perceptions of things and objects that appear to be given. This is precisely the programme of phenomenology that is of such crucial importance to modern cognitive science: to investigate, without prejudice and rash judgment, our experiences and perceptions, to include ourselves as scientists in our reflections, in order to avoid any disembodied, purely abstract, analysis.

Poerksen: But if we, as you suggest, begin with our perceptions and experiences, we immediately see: there is a subject and an object. Both appear separated. That is the fundamental insight we gain. It should actually lead us back to realism again.

Varela: You are now speaking of common, everyday experience, which is formed and shaped by a whole set of theories and metaphysical presumptions. I do not propose to trust that kind of experience. On the contrary, it is the very duty of philosophy and natural science to question and challenge ordinary perception and everything that seems self-evident, and to confront it with new approaches. These may contradict *common sense* but that is no problem for me at all and quite irrelevant; the crucial question is whether they fit, whether they are true. The reference to common sense does not prove anything.

Poerksen: What do you mean by "fitting," "true" approaches? If truth is the goal of your researches, then you definitely assume a realist position, after all. Of course, there are people who believe that we could keep truth as a kind of ideal and a distant goal because we can never do more than approximate it step by step, anyway. But that thesis seems contradictory to me, too. If we want to establish whether we have achieved some partial understanding of the absolute or come closer to the truth, we must be able to compare our partial understanding with absolute truth itself. However, this comparison of realities presupposes the possibility of apprehending absolute truth — otherwise the claim of its approximation remains undecidable. My thesis is that we can only maintain the idea of truth as a goal of human knowing, however distant, if we assume an extreme realist position at the same time.

From necessity to possibility

Varela: The attempt to characterise my position as clandestine realism and a masked belief in truth is due to the definitional decision you have taken, which I certainly do not accept. You are working with a concept of truth that is based on correspondence: truth is the correspondence between theory and reality. Such a position will inevitably make you a realist. Let me just point out that there are many ways of speaking about truth. My own concept of truth, which is inspired by phenomenology and the philosophy of pragmatism, is best understood as a theory of coherence: what counts is the consistency of theories, the coherence of viewpoints. Truth is, the motto of pragmatism proclaims, what works.

Poerksen: What, then, is false?

Varela: In a pragmatist sense, something can be false only, to put it very bluntly, if it kills you. Everything that works is true. Reconsider the example of colour perception. Birds and humans experience coloured objects; their different truths, however, are not due to a correspondence between their views of reality and reality itself, but to the mutual determination of subject and object. The perceptions of birds and humans and innumerable other living beings are all viable because they allow the continuous coupling with the world. If an organism does not develop a consistent capability of moving in a coloured world, it will, in the worst event, disappear from this earth. The species will die out.

Poerksen: But there are so infinitely many, totally contradictory, perceptions and theories that simply work and that do not kill us! Deadly failure as the criterion of falsification is a bit too vague for me.

Varela: This vagueness and the fact of lacking consent are no problem at all. All this conforms exactly with scientific practice. In contradistinction to the prejudices of some people, scientific truth does not consist in the correspondence between theory and reality. Scientific knowledge is inevitably related to the surrounding circumstances of the social world and — between virtual quotes — *the reality*. Every single object of scientific research is, as Bruno Latour used to say, a *mixed object:* it is social and it is real, it is real and it is social. When someone develops theories about DNA, black holes, or the weather, then these theories must be discussed — irrespective of any hope of absolutely valid justification and ultimate security. Then other people possibly develop contrary conceptions. So we try hard to find out which of the hypotheses work better and who has the more convincing arguments. And one day new and completely different considerations and theories enter the debate.

Poerksen: Pursuing the idea of ultimate failure and final falsification a little further, we might say: the loss of life in a final conflict with the real world tells us that our assumptions were wrong. In a similar vein, Warren S. McCulloch, one of the father figures of cybernetics, once said that the acme of knowledge was to have proved a hypothesis wrong.

Varela: I would never talk like that simply for aesthetic reasons because the central images of such formulations are conflict and struggle. When I explain that individual organisms bring forth their world, and that all the different views of the world are equally true and viable, conflict and struggle lose their importance. Falsification is no longer the central concern of scientific work. There arises a panorama of coexistence, a dialogical space in the world and in science. We can find joy and fun in comparing the plethora of possible forms of existence and the diversity of views and assumptions, we can develop ideas, exchange and debate them. Absolute reality, in my eyes, does not dictate the laws we have to obey. It is the patricharchal perspective to proclaim the truth and to decree absolutely valid rules that constrain, limit, and eradicate opportunities. What might be called absolute reality, tends to appear to me as a feminine matrix, whose fundamental quality is the opening up of possibilities.

Poerksen: What is not impossible is possible?

Varela: Exactly. And what is not prohibited is permitted. There are natural limits but there is no densely woven, blocking, and stifling system of rules. This is the soft and space-creating quality of a feminine matrix.

Poerksen: Can you reconstruct how you broke through to this different understanding of cognition and life processes? What inspired your criticism of conventional scientific practice, of mainstream cognitive science, and of classical epistemology?

Varela: When I was studying at Harvard as a young man and writing my thesis, I felt dissatisfied with the prevailing discourse of representationism, with the computational model of mind, and with the dominant epistemology. Why? I am not really sure myself. At the beginning, it was probably more of a feeling that something was wrong. One reason may have been that I came from another country with a different culture and, therefore, never really belonged; in addition, I had not been educated in the standard US way. It helped, I suppose, that I really came to the USA from another planet.

Poerksen: You are referring to Chile?

Varela: Not only that; I spent my early childhood with my family in a small village in the mountains where everything I had was the sky and the animals. Life there had barely changed since the 18th century. At some later stage, I went to school in the big city, without ever forgetting about my roots, and finally won a doctoral scholarship for Harvard, one of the centres of the scientific world. The lack of belonging and the feeling of estrangement have accompanied me since the days of my birth. To appear a little odd somehow and to feel somewhat peculiar, is natural for me and provides, so it seems, quite a good platform for new discoveries and for perceptions that may seem perplexing at first. When I began to present my own views, to expose them to critical debate and to defend them, my feeling of marginalisation returned in different form. I felt myself easily excluded, appeared as a weird character to the scientific establishment, as someone who could not quite be trusted. But then I had the good fortune to meet people with whom a harmonious relationship was possible, and slowly my own perspective gained stability until it finally became part and parcel of my personality.

The theory of emergence

Poerksen: Your search for new and unfamiliar perspectives has led you, as one of your most recent books shows *(The Embodied Mind: Cognitive science and human experience)*, to combine not only American cognitive science and European phenomenology, but also to unite these two disciplines with a philosophy from the East — Buddhism — to create a new theory and a new research programme.

Varela: This combination and connection is, in no way, arbitrary or a result of personal predilection only; it is a central part of my work as a cognitive scientist. The question is for me why Buddhism should be so interesting to a phenomenologically oriented theory of cognition that treats the bringing forth of worlds. The reason is that there is, at present, a deep rift between natural science and the world of immediate experience that urgently needs to be bridged — particularly with regard to cognition. What is an investigation of our minds worth if it does not even touch on living, embodied experience? What is the point of abstract and disembodied reflection that separates body and mind into different objects of inquiry? Now it so happens that Buddhism is in itself a practically oriented, non-Western phenomenology offering a precise analysis of what human beings may experience, which is analogous to the central research results of cognitive science. It supplements, inspires, and supports the experimental approach. Buddhism — sustained by qualified techniques of self-examination — trains reflection that may be re-enacted in one's own experience and deals, amongst other things, with the essence of mind, the notion of the self, and the concept of a static and localisable identity. The weakness of Husserlean phenomenology and its central orientation towards experience is that it lacks a well-described and directly applicable method to examine experience: the techniques of Buddhist meditation as practised for 2500 years include such a method. This is the reason for uniting Buddhism with phenomenology and cognitive science.

Poerksen: How are we to understand that? Are you suggesting that cognitive scientists ought to meditate? It is hardly imaginable that the offensively rationalist science scene would accept such a proposal.

Varela: I do not care whether people practise Buddhist meditation or not. Nor am I advocating a combination of Eastern and Western thinking of whatever kind; my goal is quite simply and clearly to perform successful research. And that is why I think that all good cognitive scientists, who want to understand the mind, have to deal with the specific investigation and analysis of their own experiences and to include themselves in their reflection, in order to avoid the disembodied, abstract form of description of some ethereal mind that does not carry us forward. This study of human experience, which is gradually moving into the centre of cognitive science and is accompanied by a real boom of the investigation of the mind, requires knowledge, training, and a method; Buddhism supplies this method. Running around in gardens does not make people botanists; listening to sounds does not make people musicians; looking at colours does not make people painters. And in quite the same way, cognitive scientists who want to focus on the analysis of their own experiences and the study of the mind, must first be taught to be experts. They need means and methods to overcome their ordinary sense of reality, to experience immediately the perpetual activity of the mind, and to restrain its unceasing restlessness. The Buddhist techniques of meditation lead to experiences and insights that would be unthinkable without such methodical schooling.

Poerksen: One of the central goals of Buddhist meditation is to realise that the ego or the self — understood as some stable, localisable, and autonomous instance of control, which governs our decisions — does not exist. This very thought, however, contradicts the standard conceptions of people socialised in the West; they much rather seek the strengthening and stabilisation of their individuality. Will this not lead to a new rift between Buddhist notions and Western experiences? In other words: can cognitive science really be combined with this key idea of Buddhism?

Varela: Naturally, the ordinary mind will have great difficulty in even comprehending the idea of self-lessness. Its experience is, however, the consequence of disciplined practice, not the result of a superficial analysis of the personal self. Of course, we all assume, as a rule, that there is a stable and undoubtedly even localisable self, and that this self is the actual foundation of all our thoughts, perceptions, and actions. We believe in our identity and therefore presume a firm basis on which we stand and from which we act. When, however, the purported existence of this autonomous self is questioned, then Buddhist experience and the insights of cognitive science resemble and supplement each other. Concerning this specific question, in particular, there is no gap at all between the insights reached through meditation and the research results of cognitive science. Both arrive at the identical conclusion that an independent self cannot be detected and that the search for it inevitably leads us astray.

Poerksen: If there is no such thing as an unambiguously localisable self, how do you explain the phenomenon that we are all convinced of possessing a stable identity and an unchangeable essence?

Varela: One of the most important scientific discoveries of the 20th century is that locally interacting components, if subjected to certain required rules, can produce a globally emerging pattern — a new dimension of identity, another level of being — that optimally satisfies a certain function. This transition from locally effective rules to globally emerging patterns enables us to explain numerous different phenomena that would otherwise remain totally mysterious and impenetrable. All of a sudden, we have - within the framework of the theory of complexity and with the concept of the dynamic system — a universal key to unlock the brain, a tornado, an insect colony, an animal population, and ultimately the experience of the self. Why is the idea of an emergent pattern so interesting? Consider, for example, a colony of ants. It is perfectly clear that the local rules manifest themselves in the interaction of innumerable individual ants. At the same time, it is equally clear that the whole anthill, on a global level, has an identity of its own: it needs space, it occupies space, it may disturb or obstruct the activities of human beings. We can now ask ourselves where this insect colony is located. Where is it? If you stick your hand into the anthill, you will only be able to grasp a number of ants, i.e. the incorporation of local rules. Furthermore, you will realise that a central control unit cannot be localised anywhere because it does not have an independent identity but a relational one. The ants exist as such but their mutual relations produce an emergent identity that is quite real and amenable to direct experience. This mode of existence was unknown before: on the one hand, we perceive a compact identity, on the other, we recognise that it has no determinable substance, no localisable essential core.

Security in insecurity

Poerksen: So the self of a human being would be, for you, an emergent pattern, too?

Varela: Exactly. This is one of the key ideas and a stroke of genius in today's cognitive science. There are the different functions and components that combine and together produce a transient, non-localisable, relationally formed self, which nevertheless manifests itself as a perceivable entity. We can greet this self, give it a name, interact with it in a predictable way, but we will never discover a neuron, a soul, or some core essence that constitutes the emergent self of a Francisco Varela or some other person. Any attempt to extricate a substance of this kind is misleading and bound to fail as both cognitive science and Buddhism demonstrate.

Poerksen: What are the implications of these ideas for classical ethics where the essentialist autonomous self is invoked as the addressee of the demands of the good and the beautiful? We might claim that giving up the idea of the autonomous self robs ethics of its foundations. Unexpectedly, the actor has gone missing. The autonomous, reflecting actor dissolves into emergent patterns.

Varela: This point of view derives, of course, from the Western conception that an autonomous individual is the prerequisite of an ethical relation. You envisage an individual that interacts with another individual in an ethical or an unethical way. I do not share the premises underlying this view; they are not at all convincing and they do not accord with the latest research results and the empirical data that support the idea that the mind is not a singular phenomenon but an intersubjective one. Recent data from child development research show that the very first actions of children are not primarily intended to strengthen the individual personality but always serve to build up relationships with other people. We develop our self precisely to the extent that other people have already attained such a self; the reflection in the other makes the other's awareness our own awareness. The situation manifesting itself here recalls the relations between organism and environment, subject and object. There is mutual determination; we cannot say who or what was first. This means: the view that the mind of an ethical actor is anchored somewhere inside that individual contradicts empirical data. The mind that we ascribe to an individual is, in a most interesting sense, already of a collective, intersubjective nature. What we are, as numerous experiments with primates and also diverse neurobiological results show, is to the same extent individual and non-individual: it belongs to the sphere of intersubjectivity.

Poerksen: Marvin Minsky, too, in his book *Mentopolis*, throws out the self with the help of arguments from cognitive science, but then goes on to say that we should nevertheless hold on to the essentialist idea of an autonomous self: we must, he writes, decide in favour of this self in order to safeguard the conceptual foundation of ethical behaviour.

Varela: In response to this I can only exclaim: what utter nonsense, what inane waffle! This is definitely the worst ever written by Marvin Minsky. Can you imagine that your own ethics and your relevant moral principles are based on decisions?

Poerksen: Of course I can. Whoever acts ethically, decides, and chooses between good and bad. And this very act of choice presupposes an autonomous and stable personal self.

Varela: To my mind, such a plea for an ethics based on decisions seems absurd because I believe that my own moral principles should be based on truths that can be experienced and re-enacted. An ethics of apparently rational decisions is highly problematic both for pragmatic and aesthetic reasons; it lacks power to convince, and it seduces to moral preaching. The decision to believe something and then to act accordingly is arbitrary and unconvincing for others. It is without foundation, and it is no possible basis for ethical behaviour. However, if I take the assumption, which is self-evident, that every self is intersubjective by its very nature, as my point of departure, then ethics acquires a new basis that is no less liberating. There is then no longer any need to preach and observe commonplace moral principles, to proclaim some *know-what*, to demand rational justification or follow an imperative, but it is important to develop an understanding of non-moralist ethics together with the *know-how* of learning how to cope with situations in a spontaneous and immediate way.

Poerksen: I do not agree. If my choice between good and evil is usurped by some experiential truth of whatever kind, then every possibility of acting in a responsible way is gone. Everything is decided, everything is pre-ordained; all I can do is to endorse my truth and my scientific view of the world according to design. Ethics, in my view, presupposes the freedom and the necessity of choice — and choice requires responsibility. Basing my ethics on some truth, however, destroys all my interactive spaces with their openings in both good and bad directions.

An ethics of spontaneous goodness

Varela: What can I say? You cannot seriously imply that my conception of truth is a sort of fundamentalist *weltanschauung*, justified in some way or other. For me, truth involves the radical and maximally unbiassed observation of personal experience; it is the result of Buddhist practice, phenomenological studies, and scientific research. It is nothing final, it is not fixed for all time, but it provides a justification for my reflections of ethical questions. If our point of departure is a kind of non-essentialist identity and the intersubjective nature of human existence, then ethics can be justified in a meaningful way supported by human experience. The continual practice of self-exploration, the discovery of self-lessness and the intersubjective nature of human existence, according to the ethical tradition of Buddhism, lead to behaviour inspired by care and compassion for the fellow being. Opening your eyes will enable you to walk on without stumbling. Exploring yourself and gradually building up your understanding of self-lessness and non-individuality will enable you to make out the goal of the cultivation of the experience of interdependence. And the condition of the fellow being will turn into a matter of direct personal concern.

Poerksen: If I understand you correctly, then what you are proposing is actually to reverse the thesis formulated at the beginning of our dispute about ethical questions. You assert: the self is not the basis of ethics, at all; it is, on the contrary, a concept of division, of estrangement between me and another; it is the reason for the impossibility of real goodness.

Varela: Of course the idea of the ego or the self is of pragmatic value as long as it is not understood in an essentialist way; it helps in everyday affairs; it helps to cope with life. But if you understand your own self in an essentialist way as a territorial entity, which is firmly bounded and clearly defined, then you are forced to defend it and to fortify it — and this sense of self or ego then turns into a blockade for a desirable ethics. An identification with an essentialist self is a cause of suffering in Buddhism.

Poerksen: Could one speak about the *emergence of ethics*, in your sense as well as in a Buddhist sense? All at once, and without central control and determination, a new quality of behaviour emerges, a practice of compassion.

Varela: Exactly. The ethical qualities that emerge then are not the product of rational construction and artificial determination. The point of departure is: responsible action consists in the continual practice of self-exploration. Marvin Minsky's plea, in contrast, seems absurd: he demands of his readers — knowing full well that he is contradicting his own insights — a lasting faith in an essentialist self and the individual. Can one, I ask myself, justify a moral point of view by means of declarations of faith that one knows to be false? Marvin Minsky's moral dilemma consists in this bizarre kind of schizophrenia: one ought to behave in a way that contradicts one's own insights.

Poerksen: Such schizophrenia does not appear bizarre to me, at all. I can give you an example from personal experience that may be helpful in this connection. A few years ago, I published a number of articles dealing with the increasing aggressiveness of German neo-Nazis. In the course of my research, I met a young man who had left the neo-Nazi scene — in the face of grave peril of his life and various bomb threats — and who is now assisting other neo-Nazis in getting out. When I became acquainted with this young man, he still lived in a strongly idealogised world, was still a racist, and was still fascinated by physical violence. And yet, he was horrified by the terrible consequences of his own beliefs, when his so-called "comrades" set fire to a house inhabited by Turkish families so that the inhabitants burned to death. The death of those people really touched him. He did not give up his views immediately but he decided to get out. What I want to say is: his eventual schizophrenia proved to be the foundation of his humanity. The contradiction between his ideological truth and the decision to live and act differently in spite of it, became the basis of an ethics. It transformed a battering Nazi into a compassionate contemporary.

Varela: This example is definitely unsuitable to defend Marvin Minsky's plea. Minsky demands to believe something of whose falsity one is convinced. The story of that neo-Nazi tells us, however, that a young man realises, for whatever reasons — through intuition, an argument, or some surprising insight — that his ideologically conditioned perception of the situation is evidently wrong and untrue. I suspect that the renewed and less prejudiced analysis was the cause of the change: he parted with his system of beliefs because he had become convinced by arguments, by slowly growing insight, or by his own personal experiences.

Poerksen: But the question here is not at all whether a perception matches the facts or not. The cause for the transformation of that neo-Nazi, in my opinion, was not a new and more correct insight. The relevant distinction is not between *true* and *false* but between *good* and *evil*. This neo-Nazi changed because he realised that it was bad, that it was unjust, to kill other people, although he continued to consider them inferior.

Varela: I do not see what you mean. When that young man realised that it was not right to kill other people, he rejected and repudiated with this new insight his old belief that it was quite acceptable simply to murder allegedly inferior people.

He suddenly realised that the strangers whom he thought to be inferior were human beings, that they suffered, that they were worthy of love and that they deserved his compassion. Such an insight can only come about after a searching analysis and exploration of the situation and the self, which will then gradually change the prevailing belief. You seem to refer the transformation of that young man to some totally independent and moment-bound decision, thereby making this decision appear a wholly rational matter through which one, in full awareness, turns oneself into a schizophrenic. However, this idea of a pervasively rational and totally independent decision is, in my eyes, an illusion: one never decides; one is simply confronted one day by a change in one's beliefs. At some stage, one contemplates one's life, comparable to a process of emergence, and finds that an even more fundamental change might be called for.

Poerksen: What do you mean by saying that we do not make any decisions with reference to ethical questions? Perhaps another concrete example, one that seems closer to your views, may be of assistance here. The philosopher Hans Jonas claims, like you do, that ethics is not a matter of rational decision. His key example: you notice a baby lying on the ledge of an open upper-storey window and see it slowly moving back and forth. Jonas says: "Just look — and you know!" The impulse to rush upstairs in order to rescue the little being from falling is so immediate, so spontaneous, and so direct that we simply cannot speak of rational deliberations of any kind.

Varela: The Chinese writer Meng-tzu uses a similar example. It involves a small child on the edge of a well. Who, the taoist Meng-tzu asks, would not rush to the well and pull the child away? But Meng-tzu interprets the situation in a somewhat different way from Hans Jonas: the spontaneous, sudden insight that something which is good for others is also good for oneself, appears to him to be a general human trait. His conclusion is that we do not have to take any decision or invent any rules in such a situation. Spontaneous compassion is, he thinks, already present in all human beings. The virtuous differ from others only because they develop this experience of spontaneous compassion further and expand it to accommodate other situations; they detach it, as it were, from the very simple and extreme case of the sweet little baby threatened by death. The virtuous have managed to experience, and thus to comprehend in a very profound sense, that we are all one, that humankind possesses a collective consciousness. Such an insight, however, inevitably requires intensive training. We need to train ourselves in a systematic way to be able to assess less extreme and less clear-cut situations in order to react immediately. Buddhism even goes one step further than the Chinese writer Meng-tzu, who believes in the fundamental goodness of all human beings. If the experience of self-lessness deepens, it is claimed, then this may in itself eventually become an expression of the highest ethics, a manifestation of spontaneous, loving care, as it radiates from the Buddhas past and present. They do not radiate this love for others because they have been thinking, nor because they have decided on love, but because their whole being *is* love. The experience of an absolute reality *is* love. It is immersed in love.

Poerksen: In your book *Ethical Know-How* you also refer to this reality immersed in love. You quote the Buddhist assumption "that authentic sorrow inhabits the foundations of all Being and can be made to unfold fully through continual ethical education."

Varela: I consider this a most interesting hypothesis, not a truth that I would submit to unconditionally. I am not decided as to that, but such an assumption attracts my special attention because I have always had the good fortune in my life to meet people who radiated an unconditional feeling of loving care and spontaneous mercy. It is very moving to see how such love and concern for another manifest themselves in action — without requiring words. Finally, much of what is said in Buddhist circles matches my own modest experiences: the less I cultivate my own small self as the centre, the better I manage to care for others, the better I can listen to my children and pay attention to them and their needs.

Postmodern biology

Poerksen: How, do you think, can we reach a decision on whether there is really something like a *fundamentally good existence*?

Varela: Well, my answer will probably strike you as quite familiar: "Keep your mind open! Let us continue to look!" The goal is not at all, as Buddhist teachers never tire of pointing out, to accept some dogma without reservation; the goal is, on the contrary, to cast doubts on it and to test it in one's own experience. We must push on with self-exploration in order to be able to decide about the possible truth of such a hypothesis quite pragmatically.

Poerksen: Studying the teaching parables of the Buddhist masters reveals that their tales and stories keep contradicting conventional morality fundamentally. There is the drunken figure of the holy fool. A crazy sage appears who hacks off one of his disciple's fingers in order to push him into some spiritual experience. There is the illuminated knave who sleeps with his female pupils. My question is now: how is this absolute ethics and the unconditional, all-embracing, loving care related to conventional morality, which is primarily concerned with leading a respectable life?

Varela: I cannot really say anything precise about that because I simply do not know. However, I want to warn of the premature judgment making conventional moral standards the base for an all-encompassing devaluation and degradation. I am not at all opposed to censuring even extraordinary people but I plead for the proper expansion of the context of observation and for avoiding a fixation on isolated transgressions. Naturally, we may be angry with a master who is always drunk but we must also see his behaviour in the light of his self-effacing activities from which so many people profit simultaneously.

Poerksen: I should like to conclude with a question and a thesis. The question might perhaps — particularly at the end of this conversation — sound strange in your ears because it is directed at something like a relatively stable, attributable identity. Here it is: Who is Francisco Varela? One possible answer comes from the cultural scientist Andreas Weber: he once wrote that you are practising something like a postmodern biology. Among the characteristics of postmodern thinking, whether well-intentioned or not, are the rejection of absolute conceptions of truth and static ideas of identity, the integration of variety irrespective of traditional boundaries, a fundamental enthusiasm for the plurality of the living and for all new possibilities. Would you be content with this categorisation of what you do as a kind of postmodern biology and cognitive science?

Varela: Well, such a label does not make me unhappy nor does it disclose any extraordinary insights for me. I know, of course, that my attempt to combine diverse perspectives and research domains tends to disturb the present scientific scene. And I suppose one could, in fact, describe this integrative posture as a kind of postmodern quality. I cannot, however, identify in principle with the confidence with which the postmodern thinkers believe in the complete baselessness of all things. My love of science and my daily work as a scientist make me assume a more conservative attitude here. I am not sure, either, what label might describe me better. My teacher Chögyam Trungpa once called me an *all cheerful bridge* and gave me this name. What does it mean? He said that I was a man who always wanted to build bridges, design new connections, and combine different things with enormous enjoyment. That is correct.

CHAPTER 5

We are constructs ourselves

Gerhard Roth on the creation of reality in the brain, on a reality independent from human consciousness, and on the relationship between neurobiology and philosophy

Gerhard Roth (b. 1942) studied philosophy, German philology, and musicology, obtained doctorates in philosophy and in zoology. Since 1976, he has been professor of behavioural physiology at the University of Bremen, since 1997 also founding president of the *Hanse-Wissenschaftskolleg* at Delmenhorst near Bremen. This College is intended to be a place for the cross-border debate of questions of cognitive science, and a forum for the interdisciplinary exchange between the social and the natural sciences.

Roth's primary research interest — he is, at present, engaged mainly in brain research — is the encounter of a barely conceivable kind: the encounter between matter and mind, nature and cognition, in the brain of an adult human, an organ weighing about 1300 grams and containing between 100,000 million and a billion neurons. It is still something of a puzzle how the material substance of the neurons affects the immaterial substance of the mind (and vice versa). It is well known that the act of thinking is accompanied by a concert of firing neurons, and that it cannot, therefore, take place without a base that is located in the brain; but as yet, a full understanding of the mechanisms of this interaction has not been achieved.

The basic project, whose contours have — despite the many unsolved problems — become discernible, is committed to unravelling ultimate mysteries that do not repose in remote regions of space or in an external universe but deep within human beings. Their solution is now expected to be delivered by biology. Geneticists are decoding the human genome; neurobiologists are working on a naturalist explanation of cognition and consciousness. Therefore, Roth — director at the Institute of Brain Research at the University of Bremen — calls cognitive neurobiology, with reference to the German terminological tradition, a *geisteswissenschaft*, "of a special kind". It investigates how perceptions and mental states take place. It attempts to tackle the key question of the relation between *res extensa* (matter) and *res cogitans* (mind; spirit; consciousness) that has remained virulent since René Descartes first formulated it in the 17th century. It describes how a human brain produces the image of an external world with all its riches of sounds, smells, colours and shapes. The link between this research programme as designed by Roth and the cognitive quest of constructivism is immediately apparent: the purpose of cognitive neurobiology is to discover the rules of reality construction as they operate in an organism's brain.

The unknowability of the absolute

Poerksen: It is commonly assumed that perception is a representation of reality: the knowing mind, it is claimed, mirrors something that is external to it. You insist, however, that our organs of perception and our brains are essentially incapable of apprehending the world in its primordial, its real, gestalt. What are the arguments supporting this claim?

Roth: The first argument is that only very few events in the world can stimulate the sense organs and affect them at all. What is perceived is, therefore, never a representation of what exists but always a selection. The most ancient sense organs are probably the chemoreceptors; they are a particularly archaic equipment for the perception of the world. For organisms living in a watery environment, it is important to distinguish between food, enemies, and mating partners, to maintain equilibrium and orientation, but certainly unnecessary to know what the properties of the world as such might be. Neither are the human sense organs geared towards the exact apprehension of reality; they serve to identify happenings in the environment that are relevant for our survival. Only when the problems of survival are solved, can we start the philosophical discussion as to whether anything exists at all, or whether something exists independently from our biological needs.

Poerksen: Now we could argue, however, that sense organs have — relative to the intensity and the duration of the survival training during the course of evolution — become ever better adapted to the external structures of the real world. The more successful an organism's activities in its environment are, it is claimed, for instance, by the proponents of evolutionary epistemology, the greater the precision of its representation of an external world will be.

Roth: It is an interesting fact that most of the oldest organisms that have survived and reproduced successfully for a very long time — bacteria, unicellular and simple multicellular organisms — do not possess anything resembling a brain. The view of evolutionary epistemologists is wrong for one basic reason: successful survival, in the majority of cases, is simply not dependent on complex sense organs and a complex nervous system. Often quite primitive perceptual equipment is sufficient. However, as soon as the organisms with simple structures have occupied all the niches, brains that are more complex develop because, due to the competitive struggle, animals are pushed into environments that are more difficult to cope with: the enemies camouflage themselves; it is more laborious to find food and to recognise prey; and social and sexual relations are proportionately more complicated.

Poerksen: So the brain was originally an organ of flight and a mode of dodging in order to colonise other niches.

Roth: We might say so, indeed, when examining the course of evolution with all due calm and restraint. The increase in the complexity of sense organs and brains does not imply, however, that organisms are able to apprehend the world with a higher degree of ontic adequacy: the perception of bats, working with low-band echolocation, is tuned to fluttering insects.

These animals are not truth seekers; all they want is to catch their prey in complete darkness.

Poerksen: Are you suggesting that human perception is no better or worse than a bat's vision in darkness? Or do our images of reality indeed come closer to the absolute reality of what is given?

Roth: That might certainly be the case unless we are under the impression of a gigantic delusion — which cannot be excluded, of course. The brains of our primate relatives are not designed to attain absolutely valid knowledge of the world; we humans, however, unlike most other animals, possess the *capability of looking ahead,* the fundamental ability of presaging what will happen next. Such predictive competence sets us apart from bats or macaques and does indeed imply that our grasp of the world is of a more objective kind. The potential increase of objective knowledge would then be no more than a sort of by-product of the peculiar evolution of our brains.

Poerksen: How would you check a gradual approximation of reality?

Roth: This will have to remain a hypothesis, a reasonable assumption, no more. However, we can definitely claim within the confines of our experiential reality that it would be an enormous advantage for macaques to be able to discern what their tribal companions were planning to do within the next few hours. Macaques, however, are not very interested in the thoughts of others (unlike chimpanzees and humans); they may not even possess a *theory of mind:* they may not be able to take another's point of view so as to predict their activities. Are the perceptions of macaques less objective? The answer to this question must remain a matter of taste, which is not amenable to a final assessment.

Poerksen: The question of taste, then: are you in favour of assuming that human perception is increasingly getting closer to ontic reality?

Roth: One of my beliefs is that we are indeed able — within given constraints on cognition — to assess different or even contradictory theories as more or less valid. An astronomer's prediction of the position of a planet is either correct or incorrect; we can, therefore, say with some justification that the correct computation is a more adequate representation of the world of the planets than other models that lead to incorrect predictions. That is why I am not a radical constructivist viewing science and magic as equally valid conceptions of reality. I insist on a precise distinction between different levels of plausibility. Science is on a different plane from magic; its predictions are more successful.

Poerksen: Reviewing the first few moves of our conversation, I notice a constant oscillation between two positions. You emphasise, on the one hand, that there can be no doubt that we are cognitively constrained. On the other hand, you appear to imply that certain perceptions are more valid than others in an absolute sense. It seems to me that these two positions contradict each other.

The brain and its reality

Roth: The contradiction arises only if one fails to make accurate distinctions, in one's epistemological worldview, between metaphysical statements about the existence of the objective world, and differentially reasonable assumptions. I cannot, in principle, say anything about a world that is independent from my mind. Everything I am capable of saying is dependent on my consciousness and my unconscious. An "objective statement" in this context would indeed be a contradiction in terms. Nevertheless, it seems possible to increase the internal consistency of assertions in our worlds of experience and science by allowing ourselves to be guided not just by intuitions but by strictly regulated procedures of scientific investigation. In this way, we can reach an extremely practicable system of assumptions, which it would be simply absurd and unreasonable to call into question. When someone tells me that it is raining, I can easily check that by going outside and observing whether the sun is shining, whether there is only a drizzle, or whether it is pouring. I may ask other people to corroborate my individual perception intersubjectively in order to increase its internal consistency and coherence and to exclude possible sensory delusions. But this phase of doubt, although reasonable and significant, must terminate at some point.

Poerksen: In your books, you present the thesis that the brain, which constructs its own world, belongs itself to a world independent from the human mind; the brain, you claim, is part of the sphere of absolute and unconditional reality. How are we to understand that?

Roth: The thesis is necessary because the world of science does not admit logically contradictory statements. For neurophysiology, the basic assumption is, of course, that everything I perceive is constructed by a brain that also constructs me, my own self. To render such an assumption plausible I must presuppose the real existence of a brain that produces this experience. Although there can be no final proof, it seems most reasonable and plausible to me to posit the existence of an external world independent from the human mind, which contains, amongst other things, real brains. Extending radical doubt to the brain and its existence in reality would entangle me in contradictions.

Poerksen: I do not see why. I can argue with wonderful consistency: as a neurobiologist I formulate whatever I say within given biological and cultural cognitive constraints; the assumption of an external world that is independent from these constraints is unnecessary. I would in fact propose a contrary claim: the dualist division between a real brain and a tenuous reality constructed by that brain leads to a contradiction. My thesis is: this dualism is essentially a clandestine realism.

Roth: Let us attack the problem as clearly and logically as possible. The claim in question is: B is produced by A and depends on A; it is, however, uncertain that A exists. If I do not know that A exists, I cannot know whether B exists. Consequently, the existence of both A and B is uncertain. If I take as my point of departure my own conscious experience and the feeling and thinking instance of my self, which it would be absurd to doubt because there is no alternative, then there must also be a brain that produced that experience and the perceived phenomenal world, in the first place. This reality-producing system — namely, the brain — cannot, for logical reasons, be part of the constructed experiential world that I perceive: the author of a play cannot be part of it, except as an actor; the painter of a picture cannot be part of it, except as one of its components.

Poerksen: A consistent formulation from a constructivist perspective might look like this: we are all drifting around in a dark universe, we draw up certain projections of reality in places, we describe — conditioned by education and socialisation — a brain and its reality, and at some stage we stop. There can be no point at which I could possibly extricate myself from my world of observer-dependent descriptions and make assertions that would factually refer to an absolutely valid reality and a *brain in itself*.

Roth: But that is not the problem at all. The problem is much rather that even constructivists are compelled to make certain logical assumptions to make their assertions and pronouncements meaningful. Constructivists cannot deny the existence of an observer and of observations; they must presuppose the existence of their minds.

Poerksen: Who is this observer? Who is this consciously experiencing self?

Roth: Ultimately, of course, nothing but a construct, too. There is no self that is sitting somewhere in the brain watching the images of an external world on a screen, and trying hard to puzzle out whether these images match an unintelligible world or not. Such scenarios correspond precisely to the epistemology of subjective idealism held by many constructivists. The question how such a self constructs its own world seems totally absurd to me; this kind of view must be radically abandoned. There is no self that constructs the world and watches images in its brain; nothing exists except constructs by brains. We are constructs ourselves. I am forced to formulate: I exist, but as a state of sensation and experience, I am a construct, I am an image, only a virtual actor, a virtual world of experience for trying and testing possibilities of action, for planning a future. Such a virtual centre we call a self; it is extremely beneficial for survival in complex and strongly fluctuating environments.

I think, therefore I am

Poerksen: What do you then mean by asserting that the mind and a self nevertheless exist? What does existence mean?

Roth: To exist simply means: I exist, think, and sense myself here and now! Apart from that, the concept of *existence* cannot be defined with precision from a scientific point of view (just remember the oddities of quantum physics). To deny the reality of one's thinking and, consequently, of one's existence would be bizarre, as was already clear to René Descartes. The cultivation of total doubt would render any further investigation of mind and brain pointless and logically incoherent. However, if my own thinking is no longer in doubt I can take the second logical step and seek an answer to such questions as: where do I come from, who created me and my conscious experience, who produced me? If I do not take the view of the solipsist that I have created myself, then I must have been produced by something else. The answer of the constructivist and neurobiologist Gerhard Roth is: there is a system called the brain; it has produced me and caused my existence; and if I exist in my world of experience then that brain must exist, the brain that I can describe with neurobiological models. And then the next logical step is: if the neurobiological assumptions are correct and internally consistent, if the brain is actually present in my body, then an environment must also be assumed, with which I can interact and by which I am nourished. So there must be an environment for purely logical reasons.

Poerksen: The intellectual approach and the figure of argument you are employing are, consequently, anchored in the Cartesian "I think, therefore I am", and you then proceed to generalise this primary and indisputable existential assumption step by step and finally extend it to cover both the brain and the environment.

Roth: You could put it that way. The final remaining question is whether the assumption of a mind-independent world is inconsistent with this line of reasoning. My answer is: no, it is not. On the contrary, it is highly plausible to assume that my self is identical with a state of my brain, that this brain is an integral part of my body, that my body belongs to an organism, and that this organism is situated in an environment that is independent from my mind. Such a line of reasoning carefully evades the question whether my assertions are *objectively correct*. It rests entirely on logical inference, and not on metaphysical speculation.

Poerksen: I cannot follow the last argumentative step in the chain of your generalisation of existential assumptions. I cannot see how you finally manage to derive the claim that a mind-independent reality exists.

Roth: Well, in that case you fail to understand one of the central assumptions of both the moderate and the radical variants of constructivism: even the radical constructivist admits that it would be absurd to cast doubt on the view that there is a world existing independently from my thinking and the existence of my mind.

Poerksen: For me, utterances of this sort betray the hidden metaphysics of constructivism: something is claimed about which — according to accepted premises — nothing can be said, and then fundamentally untestable existential assertions are derived. The assumption of an unquestionably existent external world certainly sounds more reasonable and more welcoming and will certainly boost its public acceptance. All the same, against the background of the basic contentions, the assumption seems to me mere speculation.

Roth: Your criticism is fallacious. Although I may start with the admission that my claims concerning a mind-independent world are in no way absolutely certain, nobody can prevent me from speculating about the potential existence of that world and to try to develop my own ideas about it in as rational a way as possible. Let us assume that there is a mind-independent world to which we ascribe specific properties. I can then ponder what might follow from those assumed properties. As a scientist, I can make certain predictions; and I may in the end — should the predictions be confirmed — arrive at an intersubjectively plausible model of that world, which can continually be improved. Let me repeat that the only possibility I see is the optimisation of this internal consistency. Scientists, however carefully they may proceed, can do no more than to perceive observations and research data and relate them to each other. Their observations can only be checked by means of other observations; they can never extricate themselves from the world of human perception and thinking. Saying this and asserting it explicitly beforehand, entails that I cannot be classified as an objectivist and a metaphysicist.

Poerksen: Nonetheless, whoever describes an unbridgeable frontier of cognition and an eternally hidden absolute, will unavoidably inspire attempts to tackle the question of what might lurk behind that frontier. They will arouse curiosity and interest and stimulate the exploration of the unknown. Perhaps metaphysics and mysticism will regain a place in the wake of such constructivist inspiration.

Roth: It is indeed my impression that some constructivists are mystics straight and simple. Their glorification of the unknowable is the reason for my reserve and also, of course, for various disputes. I approach these questions in a much more innocent way, and I am amazed to observe over and over again how even sane people can perceive the so-called *one and only world* in so many different ways, immune to any enlightenment, and how they construct their own realities in their brains.

The language of the neurons

Poerksen: How does this take place? Perhaps the best approach would be the demonstration of a very simple situation: some external stimulus is registered, and suddenly we perceive something, we hear a melody, feel pain, or see a picture. How does our brain construct such sensations and impressions?

Roth: Only a tiny fraction of the totality of external stimuli reaches us, and only a portion of that fraction is transformed into electric activity, the uniform code of the nervous system, and into chemical messengers, so-called transmitters. The brain has produced the reality we experience and live in. The brain, however, has no direct contact with the environment, and therefore the transition from the physical and chemical environment is a radical break. Everything we see, hear, smell, think, and feel is the result of a gigantic construction performance of the brain.

Poerksen: In precise detail: What happens when we both see a picture?

Roth: Seeing a picture has many dimensions. What reaches the brain from the photoreceptors in the eye, the rods and cones, via a number of intermediate processors, are, however, only two kinds of information relating to the wavelength and the intensity of a point of light. From the different wavelengths, the brain later computes the colour of the picture; the light intensity is the source of the distinction between bright and dark areas. The impression of spatial distribution, gestalt, form, and depth is derived from the activities of many different receptors by the brain. The consequence is that there is no colour, no form, no space, no movement, no depth, and definitely no meaning, at the level of the retina.

Poerksen: You say: what excites my sense organs is not coded there in its specific physical or chemical properties but reaches the brain exclusively in the form of electric impulses and neurotransmitters. This means, however, that the motley, multi-coloured, and many-shaded world in which we live must somehow re-emerge from the indistinguishable grey of the uniform neuronal code.

Roth: It is the highly skilled task of the theory of perception to explain this. The first father of modern physiology, Johannes Müller, believed that relating the different sensory qualities and modalities to various substances that are transmitted through the nerves might solve the problem of the infinite multiversity of perception. He postulated substances of vision, hearing, smell, and taste, which on external stimulation creep from the eyes, the ears, the nose etc. through the neural tubes to the brain. The brain then assesses the incoming substances and decides: aha, a visual impression, a smell, or a taste!

Poerksen: This would actually mean that the world's infinite nuances are already integrated into the receptive apparatus of human beings.

Roth: This view inspired Johannes Müller to formulate the famous law of the specificity of sensory energy. His pupil Hermann von Helmholtz, who discovered together with his colleagues that all sensory stimulation was transformed into relatively uniform nervous impulses, refuted it just over a hundred years ago. This is the principle of the *neutrality of the neuronal code*. Its acceptance renders the multiplicity of perceptual contents very mysterious. Sensory physiology, the growing sceptic Hermann von Helmholtz asserted, would never be able to explain the different experiential qualities. However, this is an error. Our sensory apparatus, it is true, converts all the different stimuli — electromagnetic waves, odorous molecules, sound waves, mechanical deformations — into more or less identical neuronal excitations. When I record such excitations in my laboratory, I cannot tell whether the registered nerve impulse is related to smell or taste, feeling or thinking. But the brain can do that. How does it manage to create our infinitely varied experiential world from the uniform pulp of neuronal events? The solution of the puzzle: it essentially depends on the location of the impulse in the brain. If there is an impulse in the visual cortex, a visual impression will arise independently from where the excitation comes from, whether it originates in a natural input from the retina or in an electric stimulation. If the same impulse, however, reaches the auditory cortex, an auditory sensation will arise, if it arrives in the somatosensory cortex, the brain will register an impression of touch. There are comparable special areas in the brain for qualities like colour and form.

Poerksen: The activation of a particular spot causes a specific impression to arise; suddenly we hear and feel.

Roth: Exactly. The optic nerve terminates in a particular section of the brain, which is different from the terminal areas of the auditory nerves. If there were confusion, we could hear lightning and see thunder for a while, until the brain had registered the mix-up through behavioural control and rewired itself. The specificity of an impulse results, as we know today, from the *topology of the brain*: different locations of activity define the modality, the quality and the intensity of a stimulus.

Poerksen: How does this explanation fit the observation that we cannot perceive stimuli separately, that we cannot experience colour, form, and movement independently? There ought to be a further mechanism in the brain that integrates the diverse excitations into the final comprehensive impression, which might, for instance, mean: this is a big red ball flying through the air.

Roth: There is indeed such a mechanism but before it can be activated, the different sensory stimuli must first be constituted independently from each other. This is necessarily so because after the different kinds of information have been pooled they cannot be recovered again. Whenever we see something we do not only perceive the total image but we can always pick out singular impressions and details, describe particularities like colour or form etc. This means that the possibility of recognising both details of arbitrary calibre and the overall image must be available in parallel. Here, too, the brain works with distributed and anatomically clearly distinguishable centres. Some are responsible for details, others for the total view.

Poerksen: In the process of perception an event first becomes a stimulus, which is then translated into the language of the brain and processed in certain places so that it gains further specificity. Is this happening all the time; is something new happening every time?

Roth: No, at least not with adult human beings. Many details of what we see, hear, and construct as adults are not supplied to the brain by an actual process of perception but by memory. The ingenious cognitive skill of remembering is what makes memory effectively our most important sense organ: a brain with years of experience, if placed in some arbitrary situation, can establish within seconds whether it is familiar with the environment. When after a few milliseconds the unconscious feedback reports that the situation is familiar, that I am in my study, for instance, memory will at one stroke produce the image of this room. The re-enactment of the image, released by only a few sign stimuli, is far quicker than it would be if the eye had to scan the environment atomistically every single time. This is to say: the process of construction only very rarely runs through all the laborious details that I have described. It does so with babies and small children; with adults only, when they find themselves in a completely unfamiliar environment. As a rule we can, however, because of our experience, see within moments what the matter is.

The step theory of communication

Poerksen: Up to now, we have been dealing with a particular constellation: there is a clearly discernible external stimulus that is processed. In the world of thinking, however, which so fundamentally conditions our reality, such an unambiguous input is lacking; there is no clearly defined external stimulus releasing just one specific thought. How far has cognitive neurobiology progressed in the explanation of what goes on in the mind?

Roth: We know today that the wiring of the cortex that is responsible for our conscious experiences shows that it is essentially busy with itself. An excitation that is known to come from outside is followed by 100,000 excitations inside the brain; a single scrap of information is processed by 100,000 instances. Only a small number of the perceptions of adult humans are related at all to external sensory stimuli, they are increasingly taken from memory. Thinking increases this constructivity of the brain, and the detachment from external events reaches a new level: thoughts and images are clearly abstracted perceptions and derived movements. One of the sensational research results of recent years is that brain centres, which are active in the case of movements, are equally active when we see movement or even when we only imagine it. So much on the construction of thoughts in the individual reality of a single brain.

Poerksen: To what extent are the realities that we construct for ourselves, in fact, unique? You keep emphasising that human individuals live in very different perceptual worlds. Your claim is, however, evidently contradicted by observations and experiences that are easily accessible: we do not misunderstand each other all the time; we are able to meet at agreed times; we can make appointments in the future; we can, within certain limits, agree about seeing the same things. The problem arises, therefore, how our different brains and their realities have been aligned with each other, how mutual understanding becomes possible — despite all individual construction?

Roth: One of the well-justified claims of constructivism is that meaning, and information in the sense of meaning, cannot be transmitted. What we are exchanging in this conversation is sound waves to which we possibly assign different meanings in our brains. I cannot guarantee in any way that the sound waves I am producing will be given the meanings I desire and hope for. The receiver, and not the sender, constitutes these meanings. Nonetheless, under normal circumstances a certain mutual understanding will be achieved. The explanation is everything but trivial: the sound waves must set something in motion in the inner ear; the auditory system must be attuned to the specific frequencies of human speech. An ant's brain cannot construct language from the same sound waves; a dog may learn it, but the capability of speech recognition is innate only to human beings. A further prerequisite is that we can instinctively recognise and comprehend certain speech sounds — threats, flattery, moans, etc. — independently from any natural human language. Communication proper, finally, rests on a shared language, which does not, however, guarantee mutual understanding. The next building block and the next step are provided by a similar education: it safeguards the assignment of at least comparable meanings to the same words. The last step of communicative ability requires common life experience. Complete understanding remains an illusion, however, although we may expect a stepwise increase in the probability of the same words generating the same meanings in our minds.

Poerksen: Does this step theory of communication imply that we are fundamentally lonely even when we have reached the ultimate plane, the last step?

Roth: Yes. We remain locked into our own cognitive worlds. Maximal communicative understanding probably occurs with people living together for many years. Everybody knows, however, that even partners of many decades may have radically different views of the meaning of certain expressions. Every individual, therefore, not only develops a peculiar cognitive system but also an individual linguistic system. People decide about their semantic universes in early childhood — in shocking detachment from the meaning universes of others.

Poerksen: In one of his papers, Heinz von Foerster once offered an enlightening reformulation of the questions and topics we are discussing here. He called brain science the *one-brain problem*. The situation of the *two-brain problem* is represented by marriage and education: here one single brain influences another brain. The *many-brain problem* is society. My question is now: how do all these many different, individually constructing brains connect to form that strange structure which we call society?

Roth: It is not at all difficult to explain because two central mechanisms are at work here. On the one hand, it is possible, through common education and socialisation, intellectual training, feedback and mutual correction in conversation etc., to strengthen the consensual domains temporarily, whenever necessary. This is the basis and the result of all long-term interaction, of all common planning and collective searching for the solution of problems. On the other hand, we must be aware that the brains making up a society do not need to understand each other totally all the time, but only partially, and only in certain situations — if at all. When I buy a ticket from a train conductor, it is irrelevant whether he has seen any of my articles on brain physiology or whether he finds me a nice person. We must simply manage to communicate on a certain required level, unperturbed by the indisputable fact of fundamental incomprehension. But the use of language permanently suggests, of course, that we basically understand each other, that we comprehend the worlds of others, even when this happens to be untrue. However, I claim that the primary function of language is not mutual understanding. The perpetual public and private talk, similar to the permanent twittering of birds, serves mutual comforting, sedates our nervous system, and signals: we are friends, we do no hack each other to pieces, everything is all right. The contents appear to be quite irrelevant. Minimal societal cohesion is produced particularly in the form of common emotional experiences; it also results from non-verbal communication. We all yell in the football arena, we all get worked up over some scandal, we organise ourselves against some threat — and suddenly society arises.

The brain in the group

Poerksen: We see, you say, with the visual centres in the brain; perceptions are correlates of brain activity; meanings are personal. Another view proposes, however: we do not see with the visual centres of the brain but with the eyes of a group, of the social community and the linguistic and cultural world we come from. We construct a world together; meanings exist above the individual. How could your biological constructivism (the theory of the single brain) be connected with social constructivism (the theory of many brains)? They definitely contradict each other.

Roth: No, not at all. The first axiom is that everything concerning the construction of our world passes through our brains. The second axiom is, however: the individual brain of a primate would never reach full maturity in the "normal" way outside a group of primates. For us to become human requires the immediate proximity and the sign stimuli of other primates from the moment of birth; our brain craves in an elementary and dramatic way the voice and the warmth of the mother, the proximity of the father, the provision of food. We must see individual and social collective together. The individual brain needs the presence of the group unconditionally and existentially. An ape on its own is no ape, as Konrad Lorenz already remarked. And we are apes.

Poerksen: You believe that humans are apes?

Roth: What else? Naturally, constructivism with is fixation on rationality prefers to envisage an autonomous self and a glorified linguistic creature that constructs its particular reality in an act of conscious decision. We are not so very different from other animals, though. There is empirical evidence now that humans are also controlled by smells in large measure. We just do not notice because our organ of smell has no direct access to our cortex, and therefore we do not become aware of these control processes. It is now well known that the socially transmitted smells, the pheromones, strongly influence whether we find each other appealing or unappealing. In experiments, people were given batteries of armpit sweat to smell and asked to classify the various odours along a scale. The resulting, widely varying, appeal values were then used to perform a highly interesting experiment: young men and young women, unknown to each other, who had judged each other's odour to be extremely appealing, are brought into contact. It is found that they do indeed find each other extremely appealing and that they fall head over heels in love because the minute odorous stimuli have reached their brains and released the corresponding behaviour.

Poerksen: Hearing the experience of love described in this way immediately releases a humanities-conditioned reflex — and raises the reproach of reductionism. The fundamental formula of reductionism is given by the statement: Falling in love *is nothing but* the mutual stimulation by odours. Are you a reductionist?

Roth: If the description that I have just given makes me a reductionist in the eyes of certain philosophers, then I am not at all impressed but really rather pleased. All I am interested in is to establish whether a hypothesis is consistent and coherent within defined limits of knowledge, no more. People who cast doubt on the results should check them and not withdraw from the game by devaluing them. Such behaviour has nothing to do with science. What would you say if I managed to present such an experiment and to demonstrate that it is possible to calculate precisely which of the subjects will fall in love with each other?

Poerksen: I would object that your experiment and its interpretation do not adequately cover the essential dimension of the experience of people falling in love with each other.

Roth: This is correct but it does not at all contradict my fundamental considerations: we first experience many things unconsciously that only later reach our cortex, and thus enter our awareness — and then start to scream for an explanation. Obviously our mind cannot simply accept the bare fact of falling in love; it demands verbal processing, individual stories, which can, of course, take place only after the preceding unconscious decisions.

Poerksen: Does the kind of biological reductionism that you are presenting here include the activity of the human mind? One of the creators of the DNA-model, Francis Crick, once said: "The self, its joys and sorrows, memories and desires, the feeling of personal identity and free will, are nothing but the behaviour of a large number of nerve cells." Would you agree to that?

Roth: No. Francis Crick has never — as far as I know — investigated neurons in his life but dealt with other things, as we know. His pertinent knowledge is exclusively derived from reading and talking to neurobiologists. I have been investigating neuronal processes for 20 years, and I do not at all consider myself as a protagonist of a reductionist approach. What we can say today is that mental phenomena recognisably arise whenever very many neurons in an extremely complex network interact in a highly specific manner. The close correspondence between certain brain processes and mental phenomena does not at all endorse the thesis that mind and consciousness are *nothing but* firing neurons. I would never assert anything like that. A close correlation between neurons and mind does not mean identity, even though neuronal activity is undoubtedly a *necessary condition* of the phenomena of mind and consciousness.

Worlds of science

Poerksen: The history of modern science can be written as a story of continual offence. With the discovery by Nicolaus Copernicus, the earth ceased to be the centre of the universe. Following Charles Darwin's doctrine, humans are naked apes. According to Sigmund Freud's teachings, they are governed by unconscious drives. Richard Dawkins claims that we are vehicles of our selfish genes. Some people seem to be worried that neurobiology may, in the end, add to these offences: the imminent threat is the decoding of the mind. How do you come to terms with your own research goals? Do you experience them as offensive?

Roth: No, I do not. I think that modern brain research is, at present, merely confirming what people with adequate insight into the human mind have known for ages. It has been known all along that human beings live in their own small and peculiar worlds and are prone to aggression, that the unconscious control of behaviour triumphs over their conscious motives, that being in love is a matter of fate, a sort of disease. All this is not new. So why get excited? Why feel offended? Being confronted, however, with the latest findings of genetics that humans and chimpanzees are related much more closely than chimpanzees and gorillas, is indeed extremely disillusioning. One gulps — and in all the nasty dealings among chimpanzees one detects an enormous similarity to certain human ways of behaving — and vice versa.

Poerksen: One of your books is entitled *Interface Brain*. The thesis you elaborate is that the brain is an interface between mind and matter, absolute reality and constructed reality, biology and society. Could there also be, with regard to a neurobiology of consciousness, an interface between the natural, and the cultural sciences? Could the brain initiate and sustain a novel kind of interdisciplinary cooperation? Is the age of division over?

Roth: I have never believed in this division. Brain research must be supported by psychology and psychiatry. How can we possibly investigate memory without the treasures hoarded by the psychology of memory? How could you ever work without the knowledge accumulated by psychiatry and neurology? Without the research into brain lesions performed by these disciplines, we would know next to nothing about the human brain. The social and cultural sciences also contribute by investigating the influence of social rules on the brain. A cooperation with Egyptologists, German or Romance philologists, is not in sight, however, because the subject matter of the respective disciplines is too disparate. In addition, there are fundamental difficulties hindering the cooperation between these disciplines. The reason is not that the explanations of human behaviour by the natural and the cultural sciences might be incompatible, in principle. That is not the point. My criticism of many cultural scientists is quite simply that they do not practise any kind of science in the proper sense. They claims they put forward owe their existence to purely private reasoning.

Poerksen: It may be objected, however, that natural and cultural scientists are fundamentally different and, therefore, diverge in their practices of enquiry. Natural scientists, it has been asserted since the days of Wilhelm Dilthey, deal with the general, the law-like, and the immutable. Their goal is the explanation of the processes in nature. Cultural scientists are, by contrast, connected with their subject matter in quite a different way; they deal with the mutable, with phenomena arising through the historical development of human individuals and social processes; they want to understand cultural products.

Roth: My view is that there is only one kind of science, which is practised with diverse methods. There are no two essentially differing ways of attaining knowledge that may both be called science. When natural scientists make claims, they try hard to supply evidence to confirm their theses, they quote corroborating witnesses or their own investigations, adduce sources and statistics that are accessible for examination. That alone is science. You state something and you provide arguments, you expose yourself to the critical debate of qualified experts. Many cultural and social scientists, on the contrary, proceed as follows: they settle down at their desks and think up something as excitingly original as possible. Purported scientific knowledge is thus transformed into a pure emanation of intuitive claims.

Poerksen: I have the impression that you equate science with empirical procedure.

Roth: That is right. There is no science without empirical method. Nobody has so far managed to prove the contrary case. Whoever wants to achieve scientific progress must struggle for minimal consent. Without consent, there can be no science and no progress of knowledge. Otherwise, everybody is just shooting their mouths off. We therefore need procedures that are open to examination. In today's social and cultural sciences, however, which are without empirical foundation, that consent is conspicuously lacking. The persistent proclamation of differences and theses with a somehow novel and exciting ring but without any connective potential has, regrettably enough, become a career booster. Natural science proceeds differently. Natural scientists today cannot with impunity simply turn current theories upside down in order to gain heightened attention; they must produce knowledge with connective potential.

Poerksen: My worry is that your conception of science will ultimately lead to an unproductive homogenisation of ideas. If I follow you, the distribution of conundrums and the generation of productive irritations will no longer be justified.

Roth: Nobody forbids a philosopher or a cultural scientist to develop their own ideas and to voice their criticism of the results of the natural sciences — that is not the point at all. Irritations, stimulating proposals, and the revelation of contradictions and inconsistencies will always be most welcome, but they must have integrative potential and admit of experimental or logical testing. Of course, I can insist with glee that the earth is a disc and that brain and mind have nothing at all to do with each other. But I must in such circumstances also be prepared to face the strong empirical evidence contradicting such claims. You should not join the philosopher Hegel in saying: too bad for the empirical facts! That is all I am saying. Who claims to put forward scientific statements must take account of all available research and all relevant counterarguments.

The third culture

Poerksen: Pushing this plea for the orientation towards tradition and established knowledge to its extreme, you might encourage the founding of an insider club dedicated exclusively to the everlasting protection of the mutual affirmation of conventional practices. I believe, however, not just for aesthetic reasons but for the sake of scientific progress, that we should keep all the barriers and frontiers permeable and also permit entry to alleged cranks, jokers, and birds of paradise. They are indispensable for getting things moving.

Roth: I am also open to quirky ideas and crazy experiments whenever there is an explanatory gap. To explain the fact, however, that a glass window can be smashed to splinters by a stone does not require new theories, nor do I have to design new experiments or revive Aristotelian impetus theory; the splintering of glass can be explained excellently by the models of contemporary physics. However, nobody yet knows how cognition emerges from brain processes. Here we face an explanatory gap that invites creative impulses and ideas. But they must be subjected to experimental examination. If people are not prepared to undertake this drudge of experimental testing, the threat of waffle by charlatans arises, who boast their importance with verbal trickery on the circus stage of science and parade their theories on the quantum mechanical processes of the rise of consciousness, for example, or on other sparks of their imagination. And at some stage the question has to be answered how to identify the most inspiring charlatan in that crowd of busybodies. Whom should I pursue, and for what reasons, should I want to deal with some hypothesis in a more precise way? What criteria do I have? Of course, I could say: I declare this problem one of aesthetics, and I shall rush after Bernhard Poerksen because he is wild in the most beautiful manner. However, this is not really a satisfactory solution.

Poerksen: I suspect that your concept of science will be generally accepted before long. I can offer circumstantial evidence. There is a most successful war cry that is raging through the academic universe now, and that clearly and explicitly assigns those cultural disciplines that do not employ empirical methods, the footstool in the business of meaning production. This war cry stems from a book by the New York literary agent John Brockmann. He describes — with reference to C. P. Snow's thesis that natural and cultural sciences form two disparate and hostile cultures — a *third culture*. The problems originally dealt with by the cultural sciences, he claims, are now articulated within the medium of empirical scientific research. Brain research and constructivism endorse Brockmann's thesis: old philosophical questions are today being answered by scientists.

Roth: That I would object to: there are no two cultures, nor is there a third culture; there is just one and only one science, just one single culture of scientific cooperation in thought and action. It is not specific to the natural or the cultural sciences, but it is firmly anchored in an intersubjective form of knowledge production. My own field of expertise — brain research — appears to me, with reference to the German terminological tradition, as a *geisteswissenschaft of a special kind*. As a scientist, I investigate the brain, simultaneously dealing, however, with the mind, and showing that the phenomena of the mind are most closely linked to the physiological phenomena. For certain philosophers, such a research programme is sacrilegious in itself; the mind as the highest ontic state can, in their view, have only one function, i.e. to comprehend itself. Nevertheless, as a cognitive neurobiologist, who works in the laboratory, I am interested in understanding how we think, how we hear melodies, understand language, enjoy the smell of a rose, how memory functions, how my attention is directed, how the brains of a normal human being and a genius work and function. And at some stage, I firmly believe, we will be able to explain what was special about Johann Sebastian Bach's brain and enabled him to write all those incredible compositions. Such an explanation of what has hitherto remained mysterious is most certainly not a threat to a genius like Johann Sebastian Bach and his music. It does not in any way destroy its exquisite nature.

Poerksen: Speculating for a moment: will there always be an inexplicable residue?

Roth: My view is that the framework of scientific enquiry will always remain limited — and that it cannot be stretched to encompass questions that concern, for example, why I might exist on this planet as a single human being, why I am able to think, what the meaning of my life is, how the universe began. We are left with a long list of mysteries on which we cannot, however, definitely pronounce that they will remain perplexing forever or perhaps be revealed at the time of death or at some other moment. The limits to our knowledge cannot be known either; otherwise, they would no longer be limits.

Poerksen: The consequence?

Roth: The impossibility of establishing the limits on our knowledge is an empty idea. The consequence? Nothing at all. Nothing.

CHAPTER 6

We can never start from scratch

Siegfried J. Schmidt on individuals and society, on the reality of the media, and on the constructivist conception of empirical knowledge

Siegfried J. Schmidt (b. 1940) studied philosophy, German philology, linguistics, history, and art. His doctoral thesis on the relationship between language and thought, published 1968, already rings in one of the central topics of his intellectual life. The question of the different media of knowledge has remained one of Schmidt's concerns up to the present day. It is the question of what relationship with the world a specific medium demands, enforces, and permits. How can the relationship between language and the perception of the world be ascertained? What principles of inquiry govern science? How does an artist observe? For Schmidt, these are not merely theoretical problems. He began to paint while still a student, he published concrete poetry, and he simultaneously wrote — schooled by an ideal of conceptual rigour — programmatic essays that created a stir in the most diverse disciplines.

In 1971 Schmidt, who had achieved his original academic qualifications in philosophy (doctorate and *habilitation*), was appointed professor of text theory at the newly founded University of Bielefeld. He soon changed to literary theory, and in 1973 moved to a chair for the "theory of literature". In the early 1980s, at the latest, he expanded his various interests again, developed — while professor at the University of Siegen — research projects concerning television, and prepared for another change of subject. He is now professor of communication theory and media culture at the University of Münster.

In his books on constructivist themes, Schmidt always pursues a twofold objective: he tests the theory by application and simultaneously works on its elaboration. On the one hand, he uses constructivist assumptions as an instrument to investigate the world of advertising or the irritating power of art. On the other hand, he seeks to develop the constructivist framework as a whole. As the constructivist authors come from very different traditions and disciplines, and either concentrate on the individual or on the culture surrounding individuals as the decisive producers of reality, the points of view are manifold and cannot easily be reconciled. The *integrative constructivism* advocated by Siegfried J. Schmidt unites the thesis of the cognitive autonomy of the individual with the assumption of the socially fashioned human being: brain and society combine in a new kind of theoretical synthesis.

The starting operations of European philosophy

Poerksen: Doubting external reality is, in the history of philosophy, often enough connected with down-to-earth matters. For centuries, the question has been repeated as to whether the table really exists at which one sits and reflects. Does it continue to exist when I squeeze my eyes shut? Is it still there when I am not present? We are also sitting at a table and discussing the weird-sounding question as to whether there is an absolute reality that is independent from our minds and that we can know. What would you say? Is there a table? Does it exist?

Schmidt: Let me confess: this perpetual question of the existence of a table, laboured since George Berkeley, is illegitimate and implausible. For if I want to know whether this table exists, there already has to be a table in my experiential reality I can deal with. The question of whether this table exists or not is an assertion that neither adds to, nor subtracts from, existence. Where is the table just perceived when I close my eyes? Only a philosopher with an ontic bent can ask such a question; his cleaner could give him the right answer immediately.

Poerksen: Nonetheless, the question does not seem pointless to me because constructivism is repeatedly accused of denying an external reality, of covertly arguing in a realist manner, and of suffering from a disturbed relationship with reality. And such queries are unavoidably triggered by the hard ontology of tables and chairs. The solidity of the wood, the obvious resistance of the real world, which may lead to bruises when bumping into it, somehow seem to contribute to answering the question of existence.

Schmidt: This is indeed a central point because some constructivists like to distinguish between the reality of experience and absolute reality. They claim that absolute reality exists but that they cannot say anything about it, that absolute reality is unknowable. However, such an assumption will, by strict logical consequence, lead to a paradox. People who insist that they can say nothing about reality as such, are already saying a vast amount. How can they know with certainty that it is unknowable and exists independently from our minds? Concerning the problem of the table: when I, a human being, whose only accessible world is the world of my experience, postulate that the table displays absolute reality that I, however, can never know, then I am making a baseless claim.

Poerksen: You, too, once wrote: "The real world is a necessary cognitive idea but not a reality to be experienced."

Schmidt: In our discourses, we can certainly formulate the assumption that an observer-independent and unknowable reality exists. But such an assertion remains *part of our discourse*. It is hardly sensible to speculate about what is beyond our discourse because we simply cannot experience it. Why should we distinguish between an inaccessible reality and our experiential world? Of course, we can — speaking with the philosopher Josef Mitterer, whose work I am exploiting here — invent some *world beyond discourse* that is allegedly inaccessible. All I can say about that world-beyond-discourse, however, must be said in the *discourse of my life here and now,* where I speak and act. Therefore, such distinctions are practically devoid of meaning; they merge, in the end, with dualist philosophies based on apparently natural divisions between subject and object, language and world, or as just indicated, absolute reality and experiential world.

Poerksen: The fact is, though, that these dualisms have been central and formative for constructivism. Its existence depends on them, to put it bluntly. People constantly distinguish between the real world and its constructed perception, between observer and observed, between subject and object.

Schmidt: These dualisms are the momentous and unrecognised starting operations of European philosophy, which ought to be understood and treated as strictly posited distinctions. Subject and object, observer and observed, were posited as two independent starting units when philosophy was born; subsequently one was forced to relate them in some way, usually favouring one side of the distinction above the other. It was tacitly assumed that such a distinction between subject and object, language and world, mind and being etc. was actually given. Some authors gave priority to the subject, others to the object; correspondingly, subject philosophies and object philosophies were developed and the fact that we produced these distinctions ourselves was conveniently forgotten.

Poerksen: This would mean that the difference between constructivism and its main rival — realism — has merely to do with the direction of thinking. The constructivist says: the observer rules; the observer constructs the objects. The realist claims: the objects affect the observer in a direct way; our images of reality are the consequence and the expression of the observed. Constructivism, if I understand you correctly, merely reverses the direction of thinking, but both realism and constructivism are dualist conceptions and diligently distinguish between subject and object. My question is now: What are you suggesting? Should we give up distinctions entirely?

Cultural programmes

Schmidt: No, that is not the point. It would not be feasible, anyway. According to what we know we can only operate with distinctions, i.e. we are not in a position to do without them. Nevertheless, we may very well ask whether these distinctions and the divisions derived from them are necessary and inevitable. In a consistent non-dualist perspective, we do not presume the existence of any distinction but attempt to derive the dualisms from what we actually observe. The question posed is: what makes us accept this or that distinction as a starting operation? In this way, ontology disappears from our assumptions and presuppositions — and the process becomes decisive.

Poerksen: You separate distinctions and divisions. Why?

Schmidt: I owe this suggestion to Rodrigo Jokisch. He does not put divisions at the beginning because divisions — he argues — always show a preference for one side as opposed to the other. For Jokisch, a division is fundamentally a derived operation; he therefore begins with the level of neutral and general distinctions both sides of which are equivalent, and from there proceeds to divisions, where one side is divided up into a relevant and an irrelevant division. In the philosophy of stories and discourses I am now working on, I make use of this suggestion and set out from neutral distinctions which are transformed into divisions in actual situations, i.e. whenever there is talk and action. Then one side of the distinction is favoured and preferred. This means: on a very general level, we have a neutral system of distinctions, which I call a model of reality. It includes the entire system of distinctions we operate with as observers, distinctions like *light* and *dark, poor* and *rich, powerful* and *powerless, young* and *old, man* and *woman*. They fixate potential positions in the field of societal models of reality. However: it is not yet laid down what they mean; they must be interpreted. The interpretation of the huge network of distinctions is provided by a semantic programme — which I call culture. Culture, in this understanding, is not restricted to art and beautiful things but is meant to interpret the reality model of a society semantically. The knowledge of how to apply this cultural programme according to expectation and how to relate the different distinctions is acquired in the process of socialisation.

Poerksen: Could you elucidate this culture-related model of reality construction by means of an example?

Schmidt: Let us take the distinction between man and woman. Processing the division further on the level of practical action leads to the question: Which is favoured? Man or woman? And when this is decided, then I can observe men or women by means of other divisions — describing them accordingly, for instance, as *beautiful* or *ugly, strong* or *weak, dependent* or *independent, reliable* or *capricious, moral* or *immoral*. They are the specific semantic attributions of these divisions, which are expressed in particular stories and discourses: in fashion and in novels, in pictures and dress codes, in etiquette and legal titles.

Poerksen: In many of your books, you have strongly relied on the work of constructivist biologists, who tend to consider individuals, in an absolutist way, as the more or less autonomous constructors of their own realities. Now you say that culture is decisive, i.e. you assume a certain permeability and receptivity of human individuals to external social influences. How has this change of view come about?

Schmidt: I am certainly not intending to create a new battle front line by now describing culture as the only decisive determinant of knowledge. This would be a misunderstanding and a renewed polarisation that would in no way help us move forward. The capital that can be drawn from cultivating bias has been exhausted down to the dregs. The question of what influences condition the construction of realities simply cannot be answered from the isolated terrains of either biology or the sociology of knowledge. A comprehensive view is required, which relates individual and society in a conception with total processual orientation; I plead therefore, as it were, for an *integrative constructivism* that unites the three components (brain and body, history and discourse, model of reality and culture). They are all involved in the construction of reality and together form a set of forces that, for analytical reasons, may be divided into a micro-, a meso-, and a macro-level. This division allows for the clear specification of the chosen perspective of observation and the particular research interest when describing models of reality and cultural programmes, stories and discourses, or even body and brain. On the macro-level, the focus is on the dynamic relations between models of reality and cultural programmes. On the meso-level, the macro-level manifests itself in the form of stories and discourses — representing the relations of sense arising from the world of living experience. The micro-level houses the individual actors, who — in the understanding of general systems theory — are considered as dynamic process-systems consisting of bodies and brains. These three sets of forces can only function together: they are all necessary for reality to arise.

Poerksen: From you and other constructivist theorists I have learned that *the one and only reality* does not exist but only an infinite variety of realities. At every garden fence, so to speak, a new world begins. My question is: can there still be, in this day and age, *one and only one culture* attributing common meaning to our divisions? Has it not split up into the most diverse perceptual styles?

Schmidt: There is no doubt that it has; and it already started around the end of the 18th century. If the thesis of functional differentiation makes any sense at all, then we must assume that every social system develops its own cultural programme. And that is why — according to my reconstruction — the urgent question arose around the end of the 18th century as to how the cultural programmes of the economy, of education, art etc. that were beginning to drift apart becoming partially antagonistic, could still be connected with each other. The solution of the problem was — to put it quite briefly and with a functionalist bent — to replicate a mechanism available in the economy. There money had been introduced in the course of the 18th century as a semantically empty mode of exchange. Money simply has no semantics, so human performance, talents, and goods could be calculated accordingly for their exchange values. This is the fundamental principle of capitalism: semantics out, numerics in! The cost determines the value. Society, consequently, implemented precisely this mechanism in the domain of culture — namely, the calculation of the value of all societally relevant goods by means of a neutral measuring unit. Culture came to be conceptualised in the semantically neutral terms of law, which were no longer founded on transcendence (by a divine order), on history (by recourse to tradition), and natural law (by invocation of the nature of human beings). Statute law is anchored, as Niklas Luhmann has shown with great precision, in the guarantee of correct judicial procedure. A law may be changed three times in the course of one week, but all that matters for judicial practice is that the law is applied correctly at the moment of judgment. So there is now a semantically neutral rate of exchange that permits the liberalisation of all cultural programmes with regard to their content as long as they do not violate official law — that is the only restriction. You may practise whatever you like in your subcultures but you must neither kill your neighbours nor set fire to their houses.

The limits of tolerance

Poerksen: The law thus appears to be — in this view — the last general foundation of a society that is split up into niches and subcultures.

Schmidt: Exactly. It creates coherence, ties diverging cultural programmes to unfolding individual demands. The law is the last regulative removed from discussion; its execution is not conditioned by another creed, another context of tradition, or another conception of the nature of human beings, but it is, due to its de-semanticisation, equally applicable for everybody. Historically speaking, this is an ingenious achievement — the outcome of social self-organisation, not the work of an individual.

Poerksen: Still, this common foundation of law is obviously not sufficient to guarantee, or at least to promote, mutual understanding. Every subculture lives in its own and perhaps very peculiar world; there is no interaction, no mutual understanding. Only very few people seem to be able to move between these different realities and even to enjoy the permanent confrontation with new and different forms of life and thought.

Schmidt: This does not contradict the development I have just described, not at all. The proper consequence to be derived from what I depicted is precisely that societal cohesion is no longer based on understanding. As long as we observe the law, we may develop our own cultural programmes without understanding each other. The twofold strategy of money and law guarantees that societies do not fall apart even though their individual members are no longer capable of doing things with each other. The rest is private. One seeks out the partners and the parties with whom one believes to share understanding despite all improbability. The result is that the differentiation of society increases constantly and that the extent of indifference keeps growing: a world that appears incomprehensible is, and can be, met with indifference.

Poerksen: You describe in neutral terms a process of relentless individualisation, which cultural critics see as the destruction of public space. Society is said to crumble, and the public domain, in the sense of a common base of reference accessible to all its members, is said to be in jeopardy. What is your view? Do you see this threat?

Schmidt: Firstly: the emphatic notion of a public domain, as for example represented by Jürgen Habermas, has always appeared fictitious to me. There have only ever been partial public domains of differing relevance, which became increasingly differentiated. Additionally, even the so-called mass media only reach specific segments. Nobody should shed crocodile tears over a threat to *the one and only public domain*. It has never existed as such. Secondly: the fact that societal differentiation is now subject to merely formal control obviously creates specific problems. We have to consider seriously, for instance, how to deal with all sorts of fundamentalism.

Poerksen: The activities of the Scientology sect are, I think, quite a good example of the particular risks run by a society under purely formal control. To put it in your terminology: Scientology exploits the de-semanticised regulative of the law as a defensive argument. The members of the sect demand respect and tolerance — and simultaneously erect a totalitarian subculture.

Schmidt: Scientology is a business enterprise, camouflaged as a moral institution. It insists on ethical neutrality — and massively uses ethics for economic purposes. The problem — also affecting constructivism — is: how are we to cope with the observable abuse of pluralism and tolerance? Constructivist authors have repeatedly been accused of legitimating practically everything, Scientology, and Auschwitz, and the private happiness of the garden bower.

Poerksen: How do you counter the accusation that you promote a dangerous kind of tolerance and libertarianism? Is the constructivist, who wants to remain true to his principles, bound to profess moral relativism?

Schmidt: No, he is no relativist in these matters, and he cannot afford to be. He is also part of a tradition and lives in a particular phase of history, is influenced by stories and discourses. Certain norms, moral standards, and maxims are the result of a complex historical development, which has shaped the constructivist, too. Whenever something happens — people stumble, fall to the ground — we do not begin to worry and to

reflect extensively on the right kind of reaction and its justification, but we either help or we do not. It all depends on the
moral principles we have acquired.

Poerksen: Where do constructivists find the hold that enables
them to distinguish between good and evil?

Schmidt: They find their hold — as all other human beings —
in religious or moral beliefs. We have to distinguish here
between different levels of observation. At the level of everyday life, constructivists are simply not in any danger of falling
prey to relativism; here they decide like all other people on the
basis of their unquestioned beliefs. However, constructivists
can (on the epistemological level of the second order) reflect
why certain norms have succeeded — and not others. That is
the proper constructivist perspective: we observe *how* people
observe; observing has become the object of observations.

Poerksen: We do not need absolute values and principles for
moral action?

Schmidt: No. All you need in concrete situations is principles
that have proved their mettle in your history and in the light of
your conscience. We act in continuity of all previous decisions.
If you find this kind of moral tie insufficient, you are either an
illusionist or a fundamentalist; you run away from responsibility.

Poerksen: If you find, however, that on every occasion you are
free to act and decide in different ways, and conclude that your
morality is contingent, then you lose something: you deprive
yourself of the power that arises from lucidity and unconditional validity.

Schmidt: I cannot agree there. The insight that some behaviour is contingent does not lead to relativism. I can establish,
on a level of the second order, that there are alternative ways of
deciding moral questions. In concrete situations, however, as
an actor in stories and discourses, I act on the level of observation of the first order — and the contingency commandment
does not apply. Moreover, contingency at this level cannot be
used as an excuse to evade a decision. In this, I am acting as a
realist. As soon as you confuse these different levels of observation, however, you are faced with all those chic philosophi-

cal problems — and you must torment yourself with questions of whether to practise a philosophy of *anything goes*, or whether the table ceases to exist when you squeeze your eyes shut and cannot see it any more.

Poerksen: But I would still maintain that constructivism keeps stirring things up precisely because different authors often link those levels in ways that prove to be most enlivening and naturally also provoking. They connect theory and practice, everyday life and epistemology — and then proclaim: there is no ultimate truth, so nothing is secure; we invent reality, so everything is possible; absolute values do not exist, so we must stomach total capriciousness. And so on.

Schmidt: As I see it, this is one of the central weak spots in the constructivist argument. Ludwig Wittgenstein already saw that it simply does not make any sense to expect the world outside to be gone when you walk out the door every morning. As first-order observers — as human beings moving in their environments — we are all ordinary realists; we are not handling constructions but life-world routines supported by good reasons. A position that constantly doubts the reality of our perceptions would be utter counterproductive nonsense at the level of ordinary reality.

Arbitrariness and construction

Poerksen: A quote from Woody Allen: "Cloquet hated reality but admitted that it was still the only place where you could get a real steak."

Schmidt: Indeed. Steaks are plainly part of reality. And I am indescribably unconcerned by the question of whether steaks are constructed. People who confront first order observers with the thesis that their steaks are not real but only constructs, must seriously face the question of whether they are still quite sane. That is not the level at which constructivism is properly handled because it is strictly a theory of second-order observation, the observation of observers.

Poerksen: How arbitrary and capricious are — in your view — the conceptions of reality that we produce? The concept of construction seems to suggest that individuals can rig up their worldviews in a well thought-out and goal-directed way. In the same way, some constructivists have been speaking of realities being *invented* by observers.

Schmidt: This is an extremely reckless kind of rhetoric cultivated with glee by some of the old masters of constructivism. Among meticulously and seriously arguing scholars such exaggerated phraseology will produce at best nothing but an incredulous wagging of heads. And the legitimate question is raised: if individuals do and construct everything on their own, why do we need societies and environments? Naturally, even the constructivist has to point out that the environment cannot be simply eliminated; otherwise, in Niklas Luhmann's nice-sounding German phrase, the jellyfish (German *Qualle*) will collapse (German *platt*) for lack of water. And it is obviously most embarrassing and ridiculous when those constructivists who have not really come to terms with their own postulates and assumptions, have to face the legitimate question: How do you actually come by all that knowledge? This is the problem of self-application or self-decapitation: if there were unconditionally valid evidence for their theses, it would have to be precisely the absolute truths the realists have been looking for. So what is the point of claiming with such unconditional emphasis that everything is invented? I have had enough of such extremely irritating guff.

Poerksen: You must explain all the time that one cannot simply construct a beer when dying of thirst in the desert.

Schmidt: Precisely. These are the costs of a popularisation by extreme reduction of complexity, which must now be managed by second-generation constructivists. And when I attend a conference I can guarantee you that someone will come along and say: "Is it really you? Or am I constructing you just now?"

Poerksen: What do you suggest? How should the debate be changed?

Schmidt: I can non longer continue unruffled with the popular rhetoric of excitement and irritation. It has accomplished its function by moving the observer into the centre. Those who are still speaking of an *invented* reality suggest that it is something arbitrary or intentional. I firmly believe, however, that there are practically no chances of arbitrariness; we can never start from scratch, and we are always too late. Whatever reaches our consciousness presupposes neuronal activities that are independent from consciousness; everything that is said presupposes the command of a language. The construction of realities is dependent on numerous biological, cognitive, social, and cultural conditions, which we are not at all free to control; it happens to us more than that we consciously enact it. We are permanently involved in a breathless process of construction, which is empirically conditioned to a high degree. What is, for example, arbitrary about our conversation? I can only utter what I happen to have in store in my given intellectual situation. You can only understand what your history and biography enables you to understand. Where is there arbitrariness?

Poerksen: I suspect that it is the hope for salvation, the hope to be able to construct the best possible world according to one's own wishes and without any restriction, which has made constructivism so popular. Now everything depends on what substance is given to the key concept of construction. What would you say?

Schmidt: Sometimes I think that we might perhaps do better to refrain from using the concept of construction, and that we should much rather speak of reality as something emerging, as something gradually forming itself on the basis of stories and traditions. Of course, the concept of emergence is of comparable vagueness but it lacks — and that is essential — both the intentionalist and the voluntarist aspect.

A constructivist media theory

Poerksen: In a meanwhile well-known introduction — to move to another topic — you celebrated constructivism with noticeable euphoria as a "new paradigm" that was going to transform the basic tenets of various disciplines and lead to new ways of observation. You have now been working primarily as a media and communication scientist for a number of years. Could you illustrate your thesis of the innovative effect of constructivist thinking using these disciplines as examples?

Schmidt: The transformation is particularly conspicuous in the investigation of media effects. Here the recipient has been gaining central importance. In a constructivist perspective, recipients play an important role in the processing of the media offerings. For such a user-oriented approach, which has, of course, been discussed for quite some time, constructivism could really prove helpful because it keeps directing us to pose the following question: What are the features of attraction in the materiality of media products that are actually effective in a specific situation and are also actually used?

Poerksen: This radical orientation towards the recipient must entail a corresponding definition of communication.

Schmidt: Certainly. All conceptions of communication as a simple transfer of information must be excluded from this perspective. Communication is understood as a process of the construction of social meaning in the individual. The communicatum becomes an offer inviting operations of exploitation.

Poerksen: What is, for you, the central thesis of a constructivist media theory?

Schmidt: It is of fundamental importance that the relationship between the concepts of *media reality* and *reality* should be re-defined. From a constructivist perspective we can say nothing but: the reality constructed by the media is the reality constructed by the media — that is all! The question how this media reality relates to the factual reality or to *the one and only reality*, is now no more than a topic for journalists dabbling in philosophy, who still believe that it is possible to compare those realities and then excitedly assert: journalism does not represent reality at all!

Poerksen: The kind of media criticism that is based on a realist foundation therefore loses its ontological hold. How does media criticism appear from a constructivist point of view? What is its frame of reference if not the comparison of media reality with the perceptions of reality "as such"?

Schmidt: Constructivist media critics will examine the make-up of a contribution. Their topics would be: selection, staging, forms of presentation. They would — to quote an example — compare the reporting of the beginning of the intifada by the first and the second German television stations. The one German television channel showed police throwing the stones children had thrown at them back at the children. In the newscast of another channel only stone throwing children were shown. The different variants of event selection, staging, and presentation, may thus be compared; one may suspect motives: why do two different stations construct these different realities out of the same event? Why is an event shown in one particular way and not in another?

Poerksen: The well-known journalist Klaus Bresser once said: "The job of the journalist is to convey truth." This view, epistemologically identical with the position of naive realism, is — according to surveys — shared by the majority of journalists. How is one to comment this kind of professional self-conception?

Schmidt: I think we must distinguish here between this expression of a professional ethos and what can actually be realised in practice. It is perfectly acceptable that the stated professional ethic should exclude purposeful deception, shoddy research, and that it should include the best effort to convey "truth" and to make event and report correspond properly; these are ethical standards and norms deriving from the established practice of journalism, whose utility has been proved in the course of history. Every honest news editor must admit, however, that there are iron-hard rules of selection. And if journalists are aware of that then they can no longer claim with a clear conscience that they are telling people *the truth*.

Poerksen: There can be no question, however, that such an epistemological position, implying as it does constant doubt, is completely unworkable in ordinary journalistic practice. Journalists need clarity; they need the fiction of ontology.

Schmidt: Much would have been gained if journalists realised, in the first place, that they require this fiction of ontology. They would then have to climb down from the high horse of true world representation.

The production of facts

Poerksen: To corroborate this central tenet that a true representation of the world is impossible, constructivists frequently adduce empirical research results. They have therefore been accused of being naïve slaves to empirical data and of believing with unconditional devotion in the results of brain research, albeit not in the truth. The question is now: what is empirical knowledge for constructivists?

Schmidt: In my book, *Die Zähmung des Blicks [The Taming of Vision]*, I attempt to answer this question and to develop a conception of empirical knowledge from a constructivist point of view. Empirical research, for me, consists in the controlled production of facts; it has nothing to do with reality or truth; it essentially involves the strict observation of specific procedural steps. This means that empirical knowledge can only be knowledge of the world as we experience it and as we then formulate this knowledge accordingly. The facts thus prepared can in no way be interpreted according to an emphatic notion of truth. For this reason, I no longer speak of the collection of data but of the production of facts, and not of data but of facts: these facts are, from the perspective of a sociology of knowledge, something that has been made and produced.

Poerksen: So you only add the constructivist premise of the impossibility of absolute truth to the given armoury of empirical research? That seems somewhat unspectacular.

Schmidt: You may have a point there. There is no total difference between a constructivist and a conventional methodology. The initial assumptions and the evaluation of the results are, however, decidedly different. This approach has irritated some of my critics who have asked me how I could at all employ the procedures of empirical social research on a constructivist basis. My reply: I transfer only the procedures — and not their justification and evaluation. If I want to ride a bicycle, I must do it in the proper way. But this does not justify the conclusion that cycling exhausts the meaning of life for me.

Poerksen: Let me repeat the question: you are continuing to use the classical methods of empirical social science?

Schmidt: Yes. I have developed the concept of an empirical science of literature, which has a strong social science orientation. However, these methods that often originated in a positivist or empiricist context must be integrated into a constructivist framework; and we must be very careful to make quite clear that all observations will only be made with reference to this particular presupposed methodology. All the facts, however carefully produced, are — from a second-order perspective — evidently contingent. That however cannot in any way prevent me from applying methods on the first-order level as meticulously and correctly as is prescribed, and from strictly following the regular steps of the procedures employed.

Poerksen: The approximation of an absolute reality can, if I follow you, no longer be a criterion for the evaluation of research results. What then?

Schmidt: It is the quality of the procedure that supplies the criterion. It is the controllable care in the production and interpretation of facts. Facts are only as good as the methods of their fabrication, and as significant as the procedure of their interpretation. And we must remember that the hardest empirical results turn soft at the moment of interpretation, at the latest: their contingency then appears ineluctable because, for any collection of facts, I can — as is well known from the interpretation of statistical data — generate differing interpretative stories. Nevertheless, there is no alternative to empirical procedure: it tames the roaming vision; it is a sort of dressage; it obviously produces subsequent cognitive costs but also certain profits; and it therefore has its justification. Dressage and discipline guarantee the production of a kind of knowledge that cannot be attained in any other way.

The need for another kind of language

Poerksen: The question is now whether this different and novel understanding of empirical knowledge and science does not require another and a new kind of language. Reading scientific prose, it is easy to see that it is governed by rules of presentation that consistently exclude the observer: one must not say 'I', one must not narrate, one must not use poetical metaphors. The linguist Heinz Kretzenbacher once maintained that scientific writing is governed by an I-taboo, a narration-taboo, and a metaphor-taboo. Taking your premises seriously, one should be fundamentally intent on violating these taboos.

Schmidt: Taking the observer seriously obviously excludes submitting to the I-taboo; the metaphor-taboo seems equally nonsensical because metaphors constitute essential elements of scientific speech. Metaphors are bids for orientation and can be exploited for creative purposes, once the idea of objective world description has been discarded. It is of course also possible to understand any interpretation of facts, in a general perspective, as a piece of narration. With full consistency and in strict observance of constructivist principles, every utterance ought really to be introduced with general provisos like "I believe, assume, think, assert...". Such a mode of writing is, however, most laborious and produces stylistic monsters; that is to say, it has its limits. People who — like some constructivists — clamour for a new language, which demotes the hidden structure of Indo-European languages, are evidently asking for the impossible.

Poerksen: In your professional work, you use a decidedly abstract style but you do not hammer abstraction into a static, final system; you keep breaking the posture of sternness by images, aphorisms, and poems. Nonetheless, I have been asking myself: does not abstraction also make the observer invisible? Abstraction does, after all, detach a thesis from the concrete experience to which it perhaps owes its existence.

Schmidt: Scientific discourse is characterised by a tendency towards abstraction; this is where it differs specifically from other discourses. The question is, therefore, whether to give up science. Do we want to abolish the difference between literature and the science of literature — like many deconstructivists? Do we want to declare — like the misunderstood Paul Feyerabend — that there is really no difference between science and mythology, between academic practice and tribal rites? With regard to these questions I remain, if you like, a traditionalist. As long as the difference between science and non-science offers rewards and makes a difference, I see no reason to reject this opportunity of gaining insight and producing knowledge. Whenever I want to change the levels of observation in order to achieve the respective insights, I must also change the levels of abstraction. Therefore, a second-order observation requires terminological and categorical abstraction.

Poerksen: Alfred Korzybski, the founder of General Semantics, once attempted to develop a new form of language in order to demonstrate to his readers: the word is not the thing; nobody can say everything about an event; everything changes. Out of this very honourable project of a search for a new form grew, we could say with a tinge of malice, a bureaucracy for relativist thinkers. Korzybski proposed to add to every name the calendar year in small print in order to communicate constantly that persons and things change over time (e.g. Korzybski 1933). He further recommended attaching numbers to every ambiguous word in order to express which particular meaning (1, 2, or 3, etc.) was being used at the moment. This proposal is evidently absurd because it implies a kind of exactitude that is unattainable. Are we not obliged, however, to indicate in some way or other that everything can always be viewed another way?

Schmidt: What is definitely necessary is a different kind of level-headedness when positions and conceptions change. One should — and I am not saying this with a high moral tone — firmly insist that one's modes of expression, one's needs, beliefs, and experiences may change. I have often been accused of perpetually changing positions, of abandoning them, or of becoming entangled in contradictions. Many consider this irresponsible. I would counter by saying: Whoever keeps saying and writing the same thing should seriously begin to worry. On the contrary, change is an indicator of responsibility; it is not a sign of weakness but may be seen as the living materialisation of the theoretical project thinking in terms of process systems and effect relations. In this way, I can myself experience the thesis that every system is in constant motion and that every reality leads to a reconditioning of systems. Thus the thesis — ironically spoken — turns into a living truth.

Science and art

Poerksen: For many years now, you have been crossing disciplinary borders although this is considered strange in Germany and not much appreciated. You have been appointed to chairs for different subjects several times; you have been professor of text theory and the science of literature, and you are today — having changed subjects again — professor of communication science. Moreover, you have always been active as an artist: you paint, and you publish experimental literature. How do these different forms of life and thought fit together?

Schmidt: They stand in a productive relationship of mutual irritation. It is naturally somewhat stressful from time to time to familiarise oneself with new terminologies, discourses, and expectations, but the life of a crossover professional provides recurring opportunities of viewing apparently familiar things with the eyes of a stranger and functioning as a kind of irritation agent in different disciplines. My art often is really a kind of headwagging about my work as a philosopher or scientist. It has the character of concurrent observation and flows back into my scientific themes in quite different forms; it also allows me to take my scientific work not so infinitely seriously that I would be unable to laugh at it; and it permits of testing alternative paths to knowledge.

Poerksen: You said earlier in our conversation: "there are practically no chances of arbitrariness; we can never start from scratch." It seems to me that the very purpose of art is to refute such a claim: art is the attempt to realise an act of arbitrariness and freedom — knowing full well that it is essentially impossible.

Schmidt: This is also a central motive behind my own creative work, I would indeed say. One attempts the impossible with some chutzpah even though one knows it to be impossible. Nevertheless, this has a special charm of its own. Here is a modest example: a few years ago I published a small book entitled: *Alles was sie schon immer über Poesie wissen wollten [Everything you wanted to know about poetry]*. In 31 chapters, I pretend to give the ultimate information about what poetry really is. Today, I no longer know myself whether the texts in this book are quotations, paraphrases, commentaries, or pure inventions. I am fascinated by this kind of hybrid text because it entangles in the form of a cool game what I am trying to disentangle day and night in my existence as a scientist. At some point whatever seems self-evident and whatever is believed to be valid is set in motion. Moreover, questions emerge: Does poetry really exist? Does language? Is there silence? Does this author have a style? Does he still exist?

CHAPTER 7

The freedom to venture into the unknown

Helm Stierlin on guilt and responsibility in systemic
and constructivist thought, on the dialectical nature
of human relations, and on the ethos of the therapist

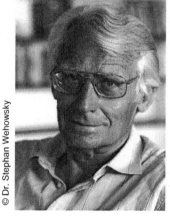

© Dr. Stephan Wehowsky

Helm Stierlin (b. 1926) studied philosophy and medicine, obtained doctorates in both subjects, and went to the USA in 1955. There he first worked as a psychoanalyst in the Mecca of analytically oriented psychosis therapy, the hospital of Chestnut Lodge near Washington, 1956-1961. He soon felt himself in disagreement with fundamental doctrines of psychoanalysis. He came to consider the fixation on the individual patient and the exclusion of family members, as decreed by Sigmund Freud himself, was mistaken because, in his medical practice, he was constantly confronted with the power of family ties.

In the 1960s, Stierlin became attracted to the early developments within the slowly growing movement towards family therapy. He designed projects of his own, conceiving of a family as a network of relations involving loyalties and delegations, and began to comprehend families as systems governed by their own specific rules of reality construction. Inspired by Hegel's central figure of thought — dialectics — Stierlin developed a particular sensitivity for the dialectics of relations, the perpetual interplay without clear beginnings, the entanglement of oppression and obedience, power and helplessness. The title of one of his books, *Das Tun des Einen ist das Tun des*

Anderen [The Doing of the One is the Doing of the Other], expresses, for him, both a research question and a programme: what people do seems to him comprehensible essentially through their fields of relations; it remains incomprehensible without taking the other into account: it would not even exist without the other.

Being trained in this kind of dialectical observation, one can recognise how the desire for closeness and the sometimes escape-like search for distance determine each other, how the power of one individual preserves the weakness of another, and how — conversely — the weakness of one person enforces the power of another.

Dialectical and systemic thinking finally brought Helm Stierlin back from the USA to the scene of European therapy. In 1974 he was appointed medical director of the *Abteilung für Psychoanalytische Grandlagenforschung und Familientherapie* at the University of Heidelberg. Since the early 1980s, Helm Stierlin has been working on integrating the systemic view, which deals with the ties of individuals, with constructivism, which postulates the autonomy of individuals. His principal interest is not the highlighting of opposites but the integration of diversity; it is synthesis, the goal of any dialectical effort.

The view of the systemicist

Poerksen: Our everyday notions of a reliable and calculable world include the assumption that reality is governed by recognisable and decipherable laws, that a cause leads to an effect in a linear way, and that we can refer any effect to its specific cause. The central assumptions of systemic-constructivist theory and therapy that you represent are, however, that there is little sense in thinking in a linear-causal way because everything is circularly connected; whatever happens manifests itself in utterly entangled chains of effect.

Stierlin: Well, I would not formulate my views in such an extreme and global manner. When a surgeon treats and cures a leg, then a certain linearity of thinking and acting is definitely required. The same applies to a rupture in the tyre of my bicycle and many other occurrences of ordinary life; we know very well there what has to be done step by step. With regard to the domain of relations, however, linear-causal thinking becomes questionable. There we realise very quickly, how profoundly cybernetics and other systems sciences have been revolutionising our understanding of living systems, and we begin to pay attention to feedback effects and processes of self-organisation. We can see what enormous effects a single impulse in the domain of relations may release: they spread within an internal field of forces, propagate itself, and generate an enormous spectrum of possible reactions.

Poerksen: One of the implications is that the consequences of one's actions become largely unpredictable: we must always reckon with surprises. What are the advantages of such an essentially uncomfortable view for the therapist?

Stierlin: A consequence and an advantage of this point of view is the new modesty required on the part of therapists. They can never know precisely what their interventions will release in other persons because those persons will process any intervention within their own systems according to their expectations. Doctors naturally use their experiences, which may help them to envisage eventual results. All the same, we can never be certain. The circular-causal view relativises the presumption of therapeutic and curative omnipotence; and we begin to acknowledge the autonomy of the patients.

Poerksen: But even as a therapist, I must keep thinking in a linear-causal way. My thesis is: you need a trivial conception of causality, raw mechanistic thinking, in fact, otherwise your actions become meaningless and completely unpredictable activities.

Stierlin: Such a conception of causality is less involved in curative and therapeutic activities than in the exercise of power and control. The questions here are: Who is going to win? Who has power? Who will prevail and with what means? The point is to impose behaviour on other persons that they must follow — unless they decide to rebel. Therapy and control are, in my view, not very closely related although both forms of intervention tend to mingle in psychiatry due to linguistic standardisation: a psychiatric hospital is by definition not only intended to cure patients, it also provides controlled protection against people whom society has defined as potentially dangerous.

Poerksen: Whenever you enjoy a feeling of pride after successful therapy, do you not refer your success to the linear efficiency of your interventions?

Stierlin: Pride is not the right kind of expression; it goes against my systemic understanding, which makes me aware of the limits of my influence. It is rather a feeling of satisfaction that one has not committed too big mistakes and that one's intervention was useful. I am indeed surprised sometimes what clients can achieve in a short time.

Poerksen: In your own practice, you often work with complete families; you do not only treat ailing individuals, but you ask parents and children and perhaps grandparents or peers to attend a meeting. Could you give an example from your therapeutic practice that might illuminate the particular character of systemic procedure?

The dynamics of self-destruction

Stierlin: Let us look at the case of an anorexic girl. It is one of the dilemmas of anorexia that the required detachment is fraught with difficulty because such families are often dominated by strong fears of separation and rigid either/or thinking. This is to say: either I am part of the family system, loved, and appreciated — or I am actually outside. With a girl that turns anorexic eventually, the individuation is often retarded; she is loving and well adjusted. In a society obsessed by dieting, and idolising skinniness, she may moreover be taunted, begins to reduce weight and develops a fanaticism of control leading to anorexia and an ultimately destructive triumph of will. Anorexic girls struggle to detach themselves, reject all food, and gravely hurt their parents, who are increasingly upset by the child starving herself to death. Anorexic persons become aware of these reactions, of course, suffer from a bad conscience but despite all carry on thinning. The entangling attachment grows even stronger.

Poerksen: Just to make the contrast to other variants of therapy quite clear: psychoanalysts probably would, when confronted with an anorexic girl, start with the game "Let´s blame the mother!" They claim that it is, in most cases, an unsatisfactory early relationship between mother and child, which causes anorexia, in the end.

Stierlin: Quite so. Psychoanalytical patterns of explanation always presume an assortment of conflicts and traumas originating at a very early developmental stage, consisting, for instance, of a rejection of femaleness and a strong attachment to the mother. Early childhood traumatisation, therefore, requires, in the view of analysts, the extensive actualisation of the conflicts through a process of transference and counter-transference.

Poerksen: What, by contrast, does the approach of the systemic therapist reveal?

Stierlin: It uncovers the entanglement; it reveals the effects the anorexic girl has on the family and vice versa. The anorexic person has two concerns: she wants to disengage herself from the parents and control her own body. These needs are satisfied in the course of the illness in such a way as to produce further effects within the system of the family. The anxiety and the angst of the parents give the sick girl an enormous power that may, in addition, release feelings of guilt; and the active control of the individual body leads eventually to an increased dependence on the medical establishment, which intervenes at some stage, treats the starvation damage, may even order force-feeding, and thus introduces total control. The girls in question often react with counter-control, hoodwink the doctors, and just drink a few litres of juice shortly before weighing. In brief: what we recognise are circular patterns of interaction, enmeshed vicious circles, which may, in the extreme case, lead to the girl's death. Anorexia, in this kind of family, appears to be the ingenious solution of an insoluble situation. The anorexic individuals radically disconnect themselves; simultaneously, however, all family members remain entangled with each other in close emotional relationships.

Poerksen: Viktor von Weizsäcker often retorted brusquely, when asked about mental and bodily illnesses: "Yes, but not in this way!" With regard to anorexia, this means: the detachment is imminent but both the form and the strategy chosen are wrong. They create a new form of dependence and intensify the relations, which should have been severed in a positive way.

Stierlin: You may see it this way, but I do not like this interpretation. It reflects the perilous either/or thinking that we must definitely overcome. The issue is neither complete disconnection nor total attachment. Both states are unendurable. The goal is to develop, by trial and error, a healthy intermediate form, which I have called *related individuation*: the ability to disengage oneself, to pursue one's ideas and ideals, and nonetheless to remain related to the parents and the family, and to keep re-adjusting this relationship on new levels all the time.

Poerksen: So how do you manage to change rigid thinking in oppositions and — if you like — the patterns and playing rules of the interacting systems?

Stierlin: Put quite generally: the willingness of the girl to change is decisive. The decision to starve must be corrected by the message that this kind of starvation is not good for the body. How to formulate this message in such a way as to make it work cannot be stated in general terms. It depends on the individual case. Some girls are very amenable to the paradoxical character and the absurdity of the situation — and can make this kind of thinking their own. Others display stubbornness and play with the anxiety of the parents. Still others can be caught with humour. From the therapist's point of view, it is essential to start out from the girl's notions of autonomy and to aim at her level of comprehension.

The question of guilt in circular conditions

Poerksen: If we transfer circular thinking to the questions of guilt and innocence, then we will inevitably start to feel slightly uncomfortable. We are forced to state: all participants are guilty somehow; each one is responsible — because all the effects are reciprocal. And if we want to be consistent, we will necessarily end up with the idea that, in reality, nobody is responsible any more. The question of guilt vanishes in the vicious circle of interactions. "Systemic thinking thus leaves behind" — a well-known therapist formulates quite consistently — "the categories of cause and effect (and, therefore, of guilt) in favour of a circular view." Would you agree?

Stierlin: Not at all. Hearing something like that immediately stirs up my opposition and a strong antagonism towards such a naive and dangerous global claim of circular understanding, which is alleged to ring in the last hours of the responsible individual. The systemic and circular view is also, quite clearly, nothing but a model that has its limits. It is only one part of the approach; the constructivist perspective, which emphasises personal initiative, personal responsibility, and therefore personal guilt, must supplement it. The more we recognise ourselves as the constructors of our relational realities, the better we comprehend ourselves as responsible for the realities we have constructed. We should ask ourselves, particularly when confronted by an image of circular entanglement: what is it that makes a difference? We are, after all, observing a game that is being played. The answer is: it makes a difference that one of the participants drops out of the game, stops observing the rules, will not rise to provocation any more, and thus violates the laws of a well worn manner of conflict management. Perhaps the entire quarrelling game is destroyed in this way. Naturally, there is no telling how such a step will affect the system of relations. But without this risk of essentially unpredictable reactions, without personal initiative and without personal responsibility there can be no progress, none at all.

Poerksen: My claim is, however, that systemic thinking forces you to abandon the idea of the autonomous individual and, consequently, the idea of personal responsibility. The individual appears in the relevant literature — I quote again — as a mere "element in a control circuit."

Stierlin: I am aware of these pronouncements, but the position I take here is decidedly different; it connects autonomy and dependence, not forcing them into an opposition but relating them dialectically. I think that you cannot be solely autonomous or dependent, solely victim or perpetrator, solely powerless or in total possession of power. Autonomy is possible only when human beings are able to reflect, at the same time, their dependence on other people, healthy food, fresh air, and a state under the rule of law that guarantees and safeguards a life of freedom within limits, in the first place. Autonomous action includes, consequently, the acknowledgment and acceptance of vital dependences. Perhaps this sounds a bit difficult. However, my claim is that autonomy becomes possible precisely when people gain an awareness of their dependence upon others and begin to reflect the consequences of their loyalty to a group or to an ideology. Moreover, we naturally come to appreciate our dependence whenever we struggle to assert our autonomy and try to question the conditions of our affiliations and our principal distinctions.

Poerksen: Those who become aware of their suppression gain freedom?

Stierlin: I believe so. It is a reflective distance that enables us to observe the causes of suppression as though from outside. And this distance renders the possibilities of freedom even more real for us; the options increase; we assume responsibility for our decisions, for exploiting or disregarding opportunities. We begin to see the reasons for our obduracy, we recognise the double binds and the impasses — and discover new domains of play and the practically infinite possibilities of interpreting the processes of events, of establishing causal chains, of creating sense, and of designing and redesigning the multiverse existing inside and between human beings.

Poerksen: You are trying to reconcile, if I understand correctly, the idea of the autonomous individual with the notion of the human being that is shaped by particular circumstances and remains entangled in them.

Stierlin: I think that we need to see both together in order to recognise how autonomy and dependence determine each other. My own responsibility and my autonomy will become clear to me only if I become aware of how dependent I am upon others. Perhaps the image of the flying bird is helpful here, the primal image of the wonderful feeling of freedom, illustrating the concurrence of opposites. Its freedom in flight is both expression and consequence of its being borne by the air.

Poerksen: It might be objected here that the understanding of the conditions of one's dependence can, conversely, be exploited for the purpose of denying and renouncing individual freedom and personal responsibility. Rudolf Höss, the commandant of Auschwitz, for instance, asserts in his biographical notes: "I had unconsciously become a wheel in the big machine of destruction of the `Third Reich´. The machine has been demolished, the motor has gone under, and I must with it." Rudolf Höss is thinking systemically here, to put it maliciously, to be able to present himself as a victim after the War.

Stierlin: This is a very good example to show a way of arguing that is widespread not only among Nazis. There are exactly these two contrary possibilities of using systemic thinking. One can — and it does indeed frequently happen — use a systemic view as a legitimating argument in order to fend off one's responsibility and personal guilt: one declares oneself a small wheel in a big machine that cannot be controlled. However, the reflection of one's dependence is also — in my view — a way of making oneself better aware of the options that are always available and of one's own autonomy so as to take on responsibility for one's actions within the limits of a finite life.

The paradox of freedom

Poerksen: I sympathise with such a view but I just cannot help finding it contradictory. If I claim that a human being is enmeshed in a certain system of relations, then I am thinking deterministically and negating the possibility of personal autonomy. If I claim, however, that individuals are free and responsible, then I must, at the same time, be negating all possibilities of external determination. Otherwise, there is a logical contradiction.

Stierlin: Systemic and constructivist thinking implies bidding farewell to the grand designs, the ideologies, and the apparently final solutions, and to face up to the risks and uncertainties of life in full personal responsibility. In this process we must also, at some stage, accept the limits of western binary logic and familiarise ourselves, as individuals acting in self-awareness, with the perpetual paradoxes of our existence where human reason founders. Total logical consistency is simply not to be had in the process of life. Lenin already abused logic as "the greatest whore": it is available for everything.

Poerksen: Perhaps anti-logic is a whore, too, and freely available.

Stierlin: Logic and anti-logic are two extreme forms of viewing reality. We must act as mediators between them and other views that are not rational. My medical colleague Ronald Grossarth-Maticek once asked 5000 academics to name their criteria of sense, validity, and truth. Scientists and scientifically minded psychologists declared that, for them, only the logical, the idiot-proof rational, had any validity. A small group of only about 15 percent said that, for them, sense and truth lay only in what they found intuitively and emotionally evident. Their motto was: I trust nothing but my affect logic! A further group, also rather small, took a middle stance between these two extremes and attempted to connect a logically founded view with an intuitive and emotion-guided construction of reality. This is difficult and complicated because such attempts unavoidably meet with paradoxes, contradictions, and inconsistencies. As for myself, I would certainly like to join the group that unites logic and emotion. I am troubled by Hannah Arendt's question how it was possible that so many Germans succumbed to the allure of power during the period of National Socialism, and why there were so relatively few that responded with purely human feeling. Where was the spontaneous reaction of compassion for the persecuted? The majority yielded to the omnipotence of a pseudo-rationality deriving from the ideological system. In this ideological system Jewish fellow citizens were a disease that had to be eliminated — without soppy sentimentality and with the professionalism of a surgeon. Here, too, rationality had become a whore due to the lack of the counterbalancing feeling of compassion.

Poerksen: Reviewing our conversation so far, I am struck by a way of thinking that is constantly struggling for a dialectical balance: you link the needs of individuals and families, systems theory and constructivism, autonomy and dependence, freedom and suppression, reason and emotion. One senses — as one of your sources of inspiration, the philosopher Hegel, would put it — a desire for synthesis, for the elimination of opposition and diversity in a new, superordinate unit.

Stierlin: Your observation is quite correct. The concept of dialectics is, for me, a sort of magical word that has fascinated and inspired me since the days of my university studies. And you are quite right: the goal of my thinking and my therapeutic work is not the immovable front, the indissoluble and unbridgeable opposition, but a kind of inspection that focusses on the individual case and primarily aims at reconciliation. This does not at all imply, however, that differences are to be blurred and contradictions argued out of sight, that everything is to be plastered up by a grand synthesis, that tensions are to be removed, and that a totalising notion of dialectics is to be employed to bring about final harmony. What is, in fact, meant is the intention to work on the concrete case and to seek to discover new answers every time, to explore the relational dialectics of a togetherness that is as alive as possible, and where new contrasts and new balances keep arising all the time. Once more: to achieve an adequate intervention as a therapist, one does not need the grand concepts or the universal directive for any imaginable occasion; what you need is the sensitivity for the individual case. Then you must act quite pragmatically.

Poerksen: You change your way of thinking according to the situation?

Stierlin: Definitely. Linear and circular causality, the models of cause and effect, the notions of individual and system, autonomy and dependence etc. are all lenses of cognition, which I apply or exchange according to the given situation. The reason for the necessity of such pragmatic choice is that these lenses open up a particular view of the world and exclude another. One must weigh up which perspective is most useful in the given situation.

Poerksen: Karl Popper and the disciples of his philosophy of science maintain that such a procedure does not satisfy the requirements of science. Karl Popper insists on the explicit statement of the conditions that might refute and falsify one's assumptions. Now you are working with theses and theories that fundamentally contradict each other; you assert the autonomy of individuals and, at the same time, their captivity in systems. The consequence is that proceeding in this way prevents failure through a clash with facts because any kind of behaviour can be integrated as possible evidence.

Stierlin: My reply to the Popperians would be: let us take a specific case — e.g. a psychosis — and apply our different cognitive lenses! What will we gain — my question would be — by observing the illness through the lens that reveals the internal conflict dynamics of the patient? What do we see when using the family lens and the systemic lens? The fact that such an approach is not based on eternally valid principles and theories seems to be a moral problem for certain people; they accuse one of capriciousness. My view is the exact reverse. The lack of complete recipes is, for me, both expression and consequence of moral sensitivity: one allows oneself to be guided by the requirements relevant to the given situation and by one's own experience. In dealing with the concrete case, the arbitrariness of a pragmatic approach with multiple lens adjustments, which is deplored by some, quickly evaporates.

Poerksen: Is there really no superordinate point of view when you are choosing your lenses according to given needs and momentary efficiency?

Stierlin: It derives from the general perspective of systems theory and the medical situation: one is always confronted with a problem that is experienced as painful. Therefore, the central questions and maxims are: what can be done to reduce pain? Might the restored well-being of the individuals and their successful self-regulation bring new pain to the other suffering members of the family? Does the avoidance of pain suffocate creative tendencies? The goal should always be to reflect the consequences for as many most widely differing systems domains as possible in order to uncover a maximum of subsequent effects.

Poerksen: Are such mobility and this sensitivity to effects learnable, or is one not bound to fail as a result of the complexity of the circumstances and the necessarily restricted capacity of comprehension? Even the grand old lady of family therapy, Maria Selvini Palazzoli, once admitted that systemic thinking is feasible only for moments at a time.

Stierlin: Systemic thinking can only be learned through one's work; it cannot be instilled into others; it needs time to gather experience and to make mistakes. Naturally, such a way of thinking is not without its risks because it introduces new complexity that in turn requires complexity reduction, which may then become the source of new hang-ups, new claims to salvation, and new ideologies.

The fundamental systemic maxim

Poerksen: Is systemic thinking not, in fact, bound to remain the business of an élite, which interferes with people's completely legitimate desire for simple orientation? Systems theory is, after all, only of interest to a relatively small circle of initiates equipped with a certain intellectual hunger for mobility.

Stierlin: What is the alternative? Should we abandon theories and the knowledge we might derive from them simply because they frustrate the craving for complexity reduction? Are possible difficulties of comprehension really valid arguments against the theories themselves?

Poerksen: My point is this: the systemic models of thinking, which expressly claim to offer universal orientation, require years of intellectual training and in due course undermine securities and destroy aspirations towards truth. Perhaps only a small number of people can stomach these consequences.

Stierlin: I cannot agree. A systemic attitude to oneself and others and the practice of self-regulation in daily life, which lead to greater well-being, are not a question of intelligence. They do not have to be connected with the understanding of a complex intellectual system. In my practice of family therapy, I am constantly surprised by how rapidly even relatively unsophisticated persons are won over to the systemic view and put it into operation for themselves with the effect of positive change. Difficulties arise, by contrast, with the intellectually refined, therapy experienced, and academically educated, Heidelberg population.

Poerksen: Is it really the other way round? Is it intuition and not so much the intellect that is needed for systemic understanding?

Stierlin: What one needs, what one should take to heart, apply, and defend against others, is above all a fundamental systemic maxim that sounds terribly simplistic: one should do more of what is good for one in the long run. There are so incredibly many people who cling to internalised fundamental beliefs and directive distinctions that force them to act right against their own well-being. They give up sexuality, they deform and twist themselves in order to win someone's love, and they struggle interminably to satisfy foreign demands.

Poerksen: Do you think that your special situation of inquiry, as practising therapist and theorist, combining theory and practice, intuition and abstraction, is particularly productive intellectually?

Stierlin: It definitely has enormous advantages because it keeps me away from the interminable and sometimes totally superfluous conceptual pettifogging of some of the systems theorists, sociologists, and psychologists. In my situation as doctor, I am permanently compelled to test the practical value of a theory. I am infinitely grateful for this constant test through daily practice; it prevents the detached and alienated playing around with ideas that I found so terribly painful as a beginner student of philosophy. When I eventually started studying medicine, it felt like some sort of deliverance; the concrete questions, the critical examination of disease and pain, and the work on corpses made me find my feet again.

Poerksen: What do you as a practising therapist and theorist understand by a system? Is it a free creation of the human mind? Or do systems exist?

Stierlin: A system is a totality, which possesses a quality that is more than the sum total of its elements. What observers accept as a system, depends on them and on the answer to the question of where the boundary between system and environment is drawn. Is a bacterium, a rat, a human being, or a family a system? Systems are, in my view, more or less meaningful observer constructs. This becomes quite clear when we consider the concept of a *problemsystem*: the therapist as observer reflects which elements make up the pain-causing system and which do not. The married partners? Must the whole family be present? Is it necessary to observe several generations?

Poerksen: Quite generally: what therapeutic methods result from systemic and constructivist insights?

Stierlin: Techniques and methods will be allotted a place in systemic-constructivist therapy if they are helpful in effectively creating differences that make a difference. They must be adjusted to the level of expectations and perceptions of the clients, and they should be judged as health improving by all the members involved in the system in question. Naturally, classical psychoanalysis also introduces differences but it remains fixated upon the narrow context of a dyadic relation; the cognitive lens is restricted to internal mental conflicts. Systemic therapists, however, embed the conflict in the relevant relational system. Their horizon for therapy and diagnosis is wider.

Poerksen: How does one proceed as a therapist in practice? Could you give a few examples?

Stierlin: One of my guiding lines is that it is impossible to formulate ways of proceeding that are independent from situations and contexts; I therefore find it difficult to give an answer. Quite generally, however: one of the most important instruments is quite definitely the technique of circular questioning. One asks, for instance, a family member in an undirected way that equally permits the search for distance or closeness, about the conflicts, expectations, and needs of another member. All the persons present are thus given a practical demonstration of the relativity and mutual conditioning of their perceptions. The goal is to stimulate mental search processes and keep something in motion, to open up new perspectives, and to increase the autonomy of every individual. Concisely: the analyst interprets, the systemicist questions.

Hard and soft realities

Poerksen: What role does language play in this process? Is it an instrument of seduction, of communication, a vehicle of reciprocal understanding?

Stierlin: All that. Whenever we seek a hold and an orientation and even a safe footing in a bottomless void, we are dependent upon language; language is, to quote Martin Heidegger, the house of being that guarantees stability. It is used to harden distinctions, it marks a supposedly static reality that is beyond doubt; it declares something proven and unshakable and serves in formulating non-negotiable positions; but it also permits us to liquefy fundamentalist claims to truth and rigidified reality constructions for therapeutic purposes. We can point to the consequences of such certainties, question them directly or indirectly, bring the counter concept into play, in order to show and present the relativisation of the original concept.

Poerksen: It might appear now that systemic therapists in their basic enthusiasm for new possibilities are primarily responsible for the liquefaction of reality constructions. Is that correct?

Stierlin: No. If irreconcilably phrased views clash, then the goal must indeed be to soften them. Questions and provocations, humour and impertinence then serve to create a new dynamics. Such an approach is often apposite when the suffering in question has psychosomatic causes. However, one can also imagine schizophrenic scenarios, where everything seems vague and fluid, unstable and undifferentiated. Here a hardening may be called for that would open up a first possibility of seeing a difference that makes a difference.

Poerksen: How do you actually do that? How does one harden a reality by means of language without marking off boundaries in a direct and linear-causal way?

Stierlin: One of the key problems of schizophrenic communication are notions of conflict that are characterised by an implacable, rigid either-or logic: there is either total detachment and complete separation, or absolute union. Given conflicts are not addressed because that would be too much of a threat. Schizophrenics tend to develop a sort of communication that keeps everything vague, shuns all determination, and mystifies everything. In such a situation, the prime target is to reach the conflict, to have it articulated. If one attempted to do this in too direct a way, one would frighten these persons and heighten their fears. Therefore, an indirect way is chosen, which might, for example, counter the schizophrenic and all-diffusing babble by an even more confused communication from the side of the therapist. Somewhere in the process a moment arrives when the client says: "Doctor, stop it now! Let us have some clarity at last! And let us get down to brass tacks, at last!"

Poerksen: Preparing this conversation, I came across these and other tricks in books by various authors, and from time to time the question arose as to whether these authors were actually good people. I was struck by a style oscillating between coldness and excitement, by a strange distance between the therapists and the people whose difficulties they analysed. What might be the reason, do you think, for being moved to asking this question of goodness when reading systemic literature?

Stierlin: I simply cannot tell you; it is your question. It is certainly possible that a kind of prose that struggles intensively for scientific legitimation and barely touches the heart will occasionally strike one as repulsive. But the other extreme would be a kind of emotional playacting as used to be extremely popular once in the scene of American family therapy; the style of some authors is also a reaction against such an exaggerated emphasis on feelings. When I study this kind of literature, I am interested to see whether the presentation is successful, whether the author has managed to translate abstract ideas into vivid descriptions and make them fluid again. And what are good persons supposed to be like, anyway? How does one identify goodness? What are the recognisable signs of goodness?

Poerksen: One feature might be that good people love human beings.

Stierlin: But what is love? These questions of goodness and love seem to me to be attempts at reducing complexity: they simplify, they supply neat formulas for extremely complex affairs.

Poerksen: The question arises then why you find complex thinking more attractive and desirable in any event. Is there a systemic key experience that you might perhaps like to describe?

Stierlin: Yes, this key experience occurred as far back as 1957. I had just started work as an analytically oriented psychiatrist in the American clinic *Chestnut Lodge*. My first patient in this clinic was a girl student who was admitted in a catatonic state. She did not speak and was completely rigid. The rigidity began slowly to recede, however, a good contact developed, and she openly talked about her conflicts. Then something very strange happened: suddenly her father appeared, took the patient away, literally overnight, and left me there in quite a daze; it had, after all, been my first case in the clinic of *Chestnut Lodge*. My supervisor, at the time, consoled me with the words that the first sign of recovery often was precisely that the parents came to take their child home from the hospital. I formed the impression then that the loyalties that keep persons tied into the system of a family are much stronger than the forces manifesting themselves in the dyadic relation of a therapy.

Poerksen: You had discovered the power of the unconscious in the domain of relations.

Stierlin: Exactly. It was this power of family loyalties and bonds, which was obviously active in relations, that occupied my mind after that experience and that I intended to use in therapy. That experience in *Chestnut Lodge* never left me and finally led me to family therapy. Some time later, I described the forces involved as transgenerational loyalties and delegations. Observing these forces from outside makes one realise that they are powerful enough to keep a patient in a state of schizophrenia.

The era of the textbooks

Poerksen: Today systemic and constructivist thinking, which was then in its beginning stages, has become increasingly popular. My question is now: might it not be dangerous both for systems theory and constructivism to gain in dominance in public and academic discourse? For me, systemic and constructivist thinking is really meaningful only as a sort of antagonistic epistemology that functions as an antidote against the arrogance of dogmatically hardened claims to objectivity. The moment it becomes dominant it loses its function. Such a way of thinking should always — put somewhat pompously — remain a *philosophy of the underdog*.

Stierlin: That will hardly be possible, but I personally do indeed regret very much that the era of the textbooks, the times of popularisation and politicisation have set in. This means that a phase of creative anarchy is inevitably ending. And one now risks becoming the victim of one's own success. The history of psychoanalysis is a cautionary tale. There is an enormous difference between the revolutionary types of the founding generation, who stood up — most of them outside the universities — against the psychiatric establishment, and the meanwhile established analytical mainstream philosophy, which now dominates the universities. I certainly do not wish this to be the fate of constructivists and systemicists. I am not unduly worried, however, as a committee of experts, consisting mainly of authors of an analytical persuasion, has just scientifically certified once again that the systemic approach is unscientific. Therapists working in this way are, therefore, excluded from the remuneration by the general health insurance companies. This is not merely a bad thing; it leaves one free to think in a non-conformist way, to venture into new things and try them out.

Poerksen: To conclude: do you think that systemic thinking might also be useful outside the therapy room? It is after all pleading more or less clearly for new ways of meeting and treating our fellow human beings and our whole environment.

Stierlin: To put it as a matter of principle: the new understanding of complex relations is accompanied, in my view, by a new kind of humility and reverence, which is changing our relationship with the world and all other human beings, and which is therefore undoubtedly helpful. I always like presenting the example of a single human finger. In this one finger alone there are 1,5 thousand million cells. Each cell contains all the genetic information, i.e. about 100,000 genes. In addition, each cell is a sort of power plant in which 2000 chemical processes take place simultaneously. In this finger alone, there is unfathomable complexity: it necessarily makes us marvel, and it cannot but inspire humility before the enormous power of the self-regulation of life. Such marvelling humility is, of course, not meant to manifest itself in a passive attitude of adoration and veneration that might eventually even lead to a sort of systemic fatalism. I am much rather concerned with a kind of awareness of complexity that meets the challenge of a reduction of complexity that preserves complexity. We must, therefore, tackle the question of what is essential with a maximum of systemic imagination and perceptual power. On the other hand, we should — in the awareness of our own limitations and with the never-flagging reverence before the enigmatic aspects of our existence — act in a responsible and decisive manner.

CHAPTER 8

Reality: we can only know what it is not

Paul Watzlawick on the axioms of communication,
on the hidden realism of psychiatric diagnoses, and
on the constructivist vision of human existence

© Peter Peitsch

Paul Watzlawick (b. 1921) studied philosophy and foreign languages in Venice. After obtaining his Ph.D. in 1949 he spent the next few years at the C.G. Jung-Institute in Zürich training as therapist and psychoanalyst. He then ran a practice of his own for some time. 1957-1960 he was professor of psychotherapy at the University of El Salvador. On the way back to Europe he became acquainted with the schizophrenia specialist Don D. Jackson and was persuaded to move to Palo Alto in California. There Watzlawick came into contact with the anthropologist Gregory Bateson and his collaborators, whose work with schizophrenics was guided by questions like: In what sense must the apparent pathological behaviour of individuals be considered adequate? What is its matching system of relations? In other words: Under what conditions does nonsense turn into sense and apparent sense into nonsense?

The primary consequence of an approach of this kind is a broadening of vision; the sick individual is no longer viewed in isolation. An individual that seems to be behaving in an autonomously insane way and in a supposedly self-governed, extremely weird manner, is seen, from this perspective, as enmeshed in an encompassing system, a family, a group, a culture. Whatever individuals do can be made to appear meaningful and consistent again within such a larger-scale frame of reference. By broadening one's vision in this way, one may recognise the pattern causing an illness, the causal circuits, and the meshes of relations, which generate conflicts and maintain them in an icy grip. Thus, the psychotherapist's room is transformed into an epistemological laboratory: the therapist seeks to uncover the hidden rules of reality construction and subsequently to right them.

Shortly after his arrival in the USA, Watzlawick started to work as a research associate of the Mental Research Institute in Palo Alto — an Institute whose members had implemented, both in their therapeutic work and in its systematic investigation, the general insights of Gregory Bateson and Don D. Jackson concerning the essential character of insane and pathological behaviour. In 1967 Watzlawick began to teach at Stanford University, was active as therapist and communication scientist, advised companies and concerns, and in his books described paradoxes and snares in communication. These publications demonstrate, in particular, the practical consequences of constructivist and systemic thinking: one realises how conceptions arise that lead to suffering, how they become rigid, and how they may be — owing to successful intervention — liquefied and dissolved again.

Theory determines observation

Poerksen: Professor Watzlawick, your book *How Real Is Real?* presents a thesis that seems to me central to all your work. In the first sentence of the book it is claimed "that the so-called reality is the result of communication."

Watzlawick: It has to be said, though, that this statement is not at all new but was already made by various ancient philosophers. They were quite clear about the fact that what we call reality is something fundamentally presumed, something created, and not something apprehended unconditionally. In the history of philosophy we can find numerous pronouncements — I only mention Immanuel Kant and Arthur Schopenhauer — that support such epistemological scepticism. Kant and Schopenhauer never tired of asserting that reality is the result of attributing meaning to unknown things. Even in theoretical physics — a field that lay people tend to consider the most objective scientific discipline — similar statements can be found. Albert Einstein is reported to have said to Werner Heisenberg in Copenhagen in 1927 that it was wrong to believe a theory to be built on observations; it was quite the reverse: it is always a theory that determines what we can observe. This is to say that the above thesis has been known for ages.

Poerksen: Nonetheless, you give this ancient philosophical scepticism with regard to the possibilities of understanding the given world a new twist. You specify what we call reality through the concept of communication. You revert the relationship between reality and communication in an amazing way, which becomes particularly clear when it is reformulated in the language of causality. The everyday notion obviously is: communication represents reality. In the language of causality: reality is the cause, communication is the consequence. This causal relation is turned round in your books: communication is the cause, reality is the consequence.

Watzlawick: You can put it this way, certainly. However, Jean Piaget already pointed out in his book *La construction du réel chez l'enfant,* which appeared in the 1930s, that the orientation of the small child, for example, was due to communications. Piaget analysed in a very careful and clear-cut way how the child creates an image of reality — and what role the communication of the environment plays in this process. The child is told, in any case: we are telling you who you are! We tell you how to view the world! Moreover, if you see it any other way you are either mad or wicked! In this way, all reality constructions are developed whether they purely personal or encompass whole cultures.

Poerksen: I think it is important to sharpen the concept of communication in order to understand in precise detail how the process of knowledge acquisition takes place and how that ensemble of assumptions is formed, which we somewhat crudely call *the one and only reality.* So: could you specify what communication is and how it colours and influences our experiences of reality?

Watzlawick: Of essential relevance to the specification of the concept of communication is a distinction by the anthropologist Gregory Bateson. With regard to a communication, Bateson distinguishes between the content level and the relationship level. The content level is the level of the apparently objective message; the relationship level, however, unavoidably adds itself to every utterance, and quite different things may happen there. This level mirrors the interpretation of the relationship, which the author of the message wants to convey, or expresses unconsciously, to the receiver. These interpretations and signals on the relationship level often cannot be spelled out in a congruent manner and may become the cause of intense conflicts. Let us take an example. Imagine a nuclear physicist telling another nuclear physicist: "The uranium atom has 92 electrons." What, do you think, will the addressee reply?

Poerksen: The nuclear scientist receiving this message might feel hurt and taunted — and might answer back: I really do not need to be told that that atom has 92 electrons.

Watzlawick: Exactly. The example shows how the relationship level contours and regulates the content level. The nuclear physicist will no doubt point out that he is not an idiot who needs to be told things like that: his answer has nothing to do with atoms and electrons; the reaction concerns the relationship level of the communication. It must be noted that this phenomenon is certainly not restricted to oral communication; it equally applies to written messages. We feel addressed differently by an authority unknown to us when reading on a door "Entry prohibited!" or "Please do not enter here!" The identical item of information on the content level is articulated in different ways on the relationship level.

Poerksen: We have now explained and illustrated two fundamental aspects of communication. A few decades ago, however, you wrote a book — together with Don D. Jackson and Janet H. Beavin — that has become extremely well known (*Pragmatics of Human Communication*), in which you demonstrated that communicative interaction is more complicated still, and that it is anchored in a set of irreducible characteristics. You called them *axioms* of communication.

Watzlawick: Indeed we did. Another important axiom, beyond the distinction between the levels of content and relationship, is that we *cannot not* communicate in the presence of another person. Even the refusal to communicate is, in fact, communication. Let me give an example again. Imagine a psychiatric clinic where you see people standing with their faces to the wall, silent and immobile for hours. Quite obviously, they do not want to communicate, but it is equally obvious that their behaviour is actually communication. A further axiom, presented in our book, focusses on the punctuation of communicative processes — or, synonymously, of *behaviour*. It has to do with the potential structure of these processes, with the problem of causality, the question of whether my behaviour is a cause or a consequence of another behaviour. How diverse and personal punctuations may be, can be illustrated nicely by a case from my therapeutic practice. In the therapy sessions with a married couple, the husband complains that his wife criticises him all the time — and that, due to this constant criticism, he habitually withdraws. The wife is annoyed and says that she only criticises him when he behaves in a cold and heartless way towards her and withdraws.

Symmetrical escalations

Poerksen: This means: the differences in the punctuation of behaviour reveal that the notion of linear causality and the unambiguous attribution of cause-effect relations do not apply to the realities of communicative processes.

Watzlawick: Precisely. Observing the interaction of these married partners from outside will make you realise that not linear but circular causality is at work there, i.e. one of those vicious circles with which we are confronted in therapy over and over again: the cause produces an effect, and the effect in turn influences the cause. And so on.

Poerksen: Are there further communicative axioms you might want to mention?

Watzlawick: The difference between a complementary and a symmetrical relationship is worth mentioning. In a symmetrical relationship, similar or identical behaviour is exchanged. Whenever one partner assumes a position of strength the other partner does the same (and vice versa). In this sense, both forms of behaviour or communication are symmetrical. The other kind of relationship is complementary: here one partner is in a superior, the other one in an inferior, position. Examples are the relationship between mother and child or between doctor and patient.

Poerksen: What is the significance of this distinction between forms or figures of relationships for communication?

Watzlawick: Whenever problems arise in a symmetrical relationship, for instance, one can observe a phenomenon that Gregory Bateson called symmetrical escalation: an exchange of increasingly impetuous and aggressive forms of behaviour. In a complementary relationship, however, rigidity — the other extreme — will increasingly manifest itself.

Poerksen: The dynamics of the arms race, which controlled the interaction of the superpowers throughout many years, would probably be an example of such a symmetrical escalation.

Watzlawick: Certainly. The Cold War is an exemplary case. One can show how the fundamental difference between the content aspect and the relationship aspect of a behaviour shapes such forms of relationship. In terms of ideal types, there are four possibilities. The ideal case is, of course, that the two partners see eye to eye on both the content level and the relationship level. The worst case is, however, that they disagree on both levels, which may result in frightful clashes. Finally, there are the two intermediate possibilities. There is, first, an understanding relationship but discord as to content. This is the most mature form of a difference of opinion: the partners in communication have different views but this does not affect the relationship in any negative way. Or the other way round: they agree about content, but not as to their relationship. After the two Big Powers had defeated Germany and Japan, all that had united them — the common enemy and the need to win — was gone. They both looked at each other, as it were, and realised that there was nothing to unite them any more. And the Cold War broke out.

Poerksen: The different axioms and variants of interaction, which you have described, enable us to draw a very complex picture of communicative processes. All the theories describing communication as a simple input-output process and as a linear transmission of information from a sender to a receiver are thereby dismissed. Our conversation started with the fundamental thesis that reality may be viewed as a result of communication. Could you now — after the more detailed description of communicative practice — elucidate how these elements and axioms of communication influence the construction of reality?

First-order reality and second-order reality

Watzlawick: As members of a family, group or culture we grow up living in and with a reality that we then adamantly view as being forever one way and not another. Quite generally spoken: we punctuate in different ways, we attribute different meanings to behaviour, and the kind of relationship and the relationship aspect influence the entire course of an interaction. The kind of relationship — symmetrical or complementary — and the relationship aspect influence what is said and how it is understood and taken in. Different attributions of meaning produce what I call second-order reality. This is the level of sense attribution and variable views of the world, which cannot be described and clearly defined objectively for all time. It cannot be decided who is right or wrong. By contrast, I call the level of actual events and indubitable facts first-order reality.

Poerksen: From a constructivist perspective, this distinction is anything but convincing. As you negate the possibility of objective and absolute knowledge, a distinction between a reality that is communicatively negotiated, and an *ontic reality*, is meaningless because, according to your premises, I can never reach what is supposed to be objectively given.

Watzlawick: Surely, you can see the trees outside the window moving in the wind, you can see the table standing in my room, the flowers with their colours on this table. And so can I. The fact that we perceive the same objects and plants cannot be denied.

Poerksen: Nonetheless, if we take seriously the theses of constructivists who base their arguments on neurobiology, it may very well be objected that this first-order reality is itself the outcome of an immensely complex process of construction, for example, the process that is required to generate the conscious image of a red flower.

Watzlawick: This is perfectly correct but does not contradict the distinction I have drawn. I am speaking about a reality conveyed by our sense organs that is seen in the same way by all the people possessing a central nervous system that functions normally, and that is first-order reality. The attribution of sense, meaning, and value is, however, a purely personal and possibly even cultural affair, though it may be shared by millions of people. To stay with the example of the perception of colour and light: even a small child will perceive a red light but it will probably not yet know that such a red light may in certain circumstances signify that a road must not be crossed. This is a pure attribution of sense and meaning, and this is what I refer to when using the concept of a *second-order reality*.

Poerksen: I think this is of central importance. You do not intend, following Immanuel Kant, to re-introduce a somewhat meaningless distinction between a *world of appearances* and a *thing-in-itself,* or to distinguish between a world that is a mere construct, and an actually existing reality. What you mean to say is, if I understand correctly, that we are always and in any case dealing with constructions of what is real, although their degree of achievable intersubjectivity is variable.

Watzlawick: Quite so. I would consider a *thing-in-itself* as nothing but one of my phantasies. How could I possibly know that this thing-in-itself exists? I hear something, see something, smell something; no more can be said, that is all. I should like to add that all we can know of that actually existing reality is, in my opinion, what it is *not*. Only the collapse of our reality constructions enables us to realise that the world is not as we had designed it. However, the failure of a reality construction does not at all justify the view that we might somehow be able to approximate that thing-in-itself steadily and step by step.

Poerksen: Now one might, of course, object that the successful functioning of reality constructions (and not their failure) is evidence of their truth. We drive cars, we telephone, and aeroplanes weighing tons rise up into the air. Surely, this can only mean that there is a systematic connection between our conceptions of the world and its true essence. In other words, and in the form of a question: Is the obvious functioning of our hypotheses not an indication that we have successfully wheedled out some of the working secrets of nature?

Watzlawick: We see an aeroplane in real flight; that is first-order reality about which we are able to reach agreement.

We possibly attach variable and culturally specific meaning to our perception; that would be, according to my distinction, second-order reality. The assumption, however, that the apparent functioning of a hypothesis is evidence for its truth seems untenable to me. Let me present an analogy here to make this clear. Imagine a ship's captain who is forced to go through a precarious strait during a dark and stormy night without any navigational aid. He does not know this strait; he has no nautical chart to help him get his bearings. There are only two possibilities for this captain. He may navigate the strait successfully and safely reach the open sea at the other end. All he knows afterwards is that his chosen course fitted the unknown reality of the strait. He was able to find a manageable passage but he does not know whether there might have been shorter or less dangerous lines of passage. If he, however, steers his ship into a rock and loses both the ship and his life, then all he can be sure of in his last moments is that his chosen course did not fit the reality of the strait and that it was not adapted to it in a way that would have secured his survival. What the strait is *really* like in an absolute sense — that he cannot ascertain in either case. And my claim is that we are all captains of this sort on our journey through life.

Poerksen: The conclusion is then, to finish the argument deriving from this analogy, that nobody can advance claims to truth in an absolute sense; we are all sailing in the dark.

Watzlawick: Quite right. Such claims to truth are nonsensical in point of theory; in point of fact, there are, of course, countless people who actually raise such claims. Just think of political ideologies, Nazism, Fascism and Marxism. Their followers have caused terrible havoc in the name of a supposedly ultimate and universally valid truth.

Poerksen: Do you want to say that terror is necessarily part of a belief in absolute truth?

Watzlawick: Certainly not; such an assertion would be nonsense. There are obviously religious claims to truth that have no terrorist or violent consequences at all. I am, however, referring to those ideologues who claim to have established how humankind must be organised to reach the final state of happiness and to realise eternal truth. The consequences can be dreadful if people of this persuasion manage to occupy positions of power that enable them to impose their truth in an authoritarian way and to bully other people on the grounds of the accusation that they are sabotaging the true view of the world. Early stages of such a way of thinking may be discovered in Plato's *Republic*, where one may read about the wise ruler's, the philosopher king's, alleged ethical right to impose his wisdom on humankind, if necessary by means of force.

The therapy of the as-if

Poerksen: Dealing with the many-voiced discourse of constructivism, one comes across diverse constructivist authors who do not take their own assumptions seriously enough and, by way of an objectivist use of language, announce clandestine claims to truth. In this way, strange and often unnoticed logical and rhetorical self-contradictions arise, and constructivism is sometimes presented as an ultimate truth concerned — paradoxically enough — with the impossibility of attaining absolute truth.

Watzlawick: Such paradoxes may undoubtedly be encountered — but they have nothing to do with what I understand by *radical constructivism*. Radical constructivism conceives of itself as a construction and not as a final truth; it is a possibility of viewing the world. For me, and I say this deliberately with reference to my therapeutic work, the only question of decisive relevance is which construction proves to be the most useful and the most humane. From an epistemological perspective, we must give up the idea that science works towards the revelation of truth; the task of science is, much rather, to develop methods that serve a particular purpose and that may be — after even only a short while — replaced by methods that are more effective. This has nothing to do with conquering the absolute truth.

Poerksen: This means that constructivist pronouncements are bound to retain this paradoxical makeup and a vacillating structure forever. In addition, I think that it is only consistent that they should be made in a flexible, open, and light-hearted manner. This is probably the only way of preventing constructivism from becoming a kind of meta-dogmatism.

Watzlawick: Perfectly correct. Today's view of things may prove useless and impracticable by tomorrow. It is simply absurd that some of the constructivists argue in a dogmatic way.

Poerksen: You have been active in family therapy yourself and have published several books that illuminate the question how change and transformation may be encouraged in a case of conflict. Could we discuss this practical utility of constructivist ideas and theories, which you keep emphasising, with regard to your own work?

Watzlawick: I have developed a technique, which I have named the *therapy of the as-if*. The concept refers to the famous book by the Kantian scholar Hans Vaihinger, *Die Philosophy des Als-Ob [The Philosophy of "As If "]*, published in 1911. On a good 800 pages, Vaihinger presents a multitude of examples to prove that we have always operated with as-if assumptions, which may be useful or detrimental. The central thing is that I always assume that a person coming to see me lives in a second-order reality, which has, for some reason or other, become a source of suffering. All of a sudden, the world has lost its meaning, the personal constructions have collapsed or are no longer functioning. I try to change these distressing constructions by interventions and to replace them by less painful or perhaps even pleasant or joyful ones.

Poerksen: How does this therapy of the as-if work in practice, if its target is merely the correction of meaning attributions that do not admit of objectification?

Watzlawick: Some company boss comes to see me and wants advice as to how he could improve the interaction with his employees, who show extremely impolite and aggressive behaviour. The way he presents himself and describes the behaviour of his employees, clearly shows to me that he himself behaves in a cold, aggressive, and impolite way towards his employees. This is another example of circular causality: a cause produces an effect; the effect becomes a cause and produces an effect again. I managed to persuade this man to carry out an experiment.

Poerksen: How was it possible to break up that fateful interaction with its incompatible punctuations?

Watzlawick: I suggested to him that the next time he had to deal with one of his unpleasant employees, he should behave *as if* the other person were terrified and had come to ask for consolation. The result of this experiment was exceptionally positive: the man acted in a less intimidating way and, consequently, his employees reacted with less aggression and . greater friendliness, which in turn made him act in a friendlier manner, too. This is a simple example of an intervention that was in no way intended to reveal the ultimate truth about the universe but only to achieve the transformation of that man's reality.

Poerksen: Could you present other techniques and methods of systemic-constructivist therapeutic practice?

Watzlawick: The fundamental principle is always the same: one begins by trying to understand the functioning of the system of human relations encompassing the suffering individual. Through conversation and the observation of the participants, who are invited, too, if at all possible, one finally manages to understand the phenomenon that the cyberneticians of the early fifties had already called the complexity reducer: in cybernetics, the complexity reducer is an incursion that does not destroy high complexity but only reduces it to useful and manageable proportions. From a psychotherapeutic point of view, one may consider the complexity reducer as the solution attempted so far: what people had been trying out to solve the problem that led them to see me, was usually precisely what kept the problem alive and made it more complicated. More drastically: in many cases, the attempted solution is the very problem. Often people think that applying more of the same solution would remove the problem, but such a strategy, in fact, only contributes to its progressive intensification. In my view, it is now necessary to find a higher-order solution, which can break through the vicious circle of interaction. The goal is a change in the here and now. This means: I reject the largely unchallenged agreement underlying classical pseudo-scientific schools of therapy, which rests on the assumption that any change in the present can only be accomplished through an understanding of causes located in the past. One must, the assumption is, search for these causes in the unconscious and in the past; one must then slowly and gradually interpret them for the so-called patients until they reach — this is the magical word — *insight*, and change. In my professional career and in my own personal life, I have never even once succeeded in experiencing or even producing this magical moment of insight.

Poerksen: You have been hinting at the various schools and directions of psychoanalysis. Is it the fixation upon an intellectual discussion and the idea of the present being determined by the past, which provokes your criticism of classical psychoanalysis?

Watzlawick: Yes; and I want to add at once that I received a complete training in Jungian analysis myself. One must state it quite clearly: the assumption that a change in the present can only be induced by understanding the past is — using the concept introduced by Karl Popper — a *self-immunising proposition.* It is an assumption the validity and truth of which is "proved" both by its success and its failure, an assumption, therefore, that is immune to refutation. If the condition of the patient improves, this is a clear proof of the correctness of the assumption. However, if the condition of the patient does not improve, despite intensive searching of the past, then this can only mean that the search for past causes has not been pushed far and deep enough; the proposition always wins, and its defenders are apparently always right.

Poerksen: If we do not assign primary status to insight, as you suggest, but attempt to change a destructive interaction by means of insufficiently transparent interventions, then another kind of objection may be at hand: one might say that you practise manipulation.

Watzlawick: To this I can only reply: can you, please, present a single example of an act of care that is not manipulative? Every surgeon that removes an inflamed appendix is a manipulator. Rescuing drowning persons means manipulating them.

Poerksen: But the degree of insight into what is actually happening is surely different whether my appendix is removed or whether I am thrown a lifeline. The persons coming to see a therapist are given new rules for living with other people, which are incomprehensible to them.

Watzlawick: When my doctor prescribes a medicine whose precise effect I do not understand, I shall swallow it nevertheless because I know that the doctor wants to help me. I can only repeat: there is, in my opinion, no difference between caring and manipulation.

The woman who was never schizophrenic

Poerksen: Perhaps this is the right moment, after our discussion of the methods of systemic-constructivist psychotherapy, to move on to another topic, which also touches your professional domain. The question is what the notion of mental health might mean in your epistemological perspective. Or the other way round: whenever psychiatrists say that hallucinating patients have lost their "connection with reality ", they indicate that their diagnostic concepts are ontologically contaminated. Implicitly, they believe in a reality that can be known and can therefore serve as the foundation of their diagnoses.

Watzlawick: Quite right. Such diagnoses rest on the perfectly fictitious belief that objective reality is accessible to the mentally healthy person — primarily, of course, to the therapist. In this way, the adaptation to reality becomes the prime criterion of human cognitive and mental normality. It stands to reason that this criterion is, from an epistemological point of view, an absurd dogma.

Poerksen: This implies that you have to use another kind of language to talk about patients and their symptoms.

Watzlawick: I do not speak about patients any more; the people coming to see me are clients. In addition, my colleagues and I no longer use diagnostic terms, no longer talk about symptoms, and use all the clinical terminology — neurosis, psychosis, etc. — only on the forms of the insurance companies. The founder of General Semantics, Alfred Korzybski, kept reiterating: the name is not the thing; the map is not the territory. It is a popular and naive error to believe that simply because there is a name for a mental illness, this illness actually exists.

Poerksen: But is not the multitude of empirical observations carrying pathologising labels evidence for the actual existence of "real things," real diseases?

Watzlawick: No. It is complete nonsense to believe that, in the area of the psychology, we are dealing with pathologies that are unambiguous in the same way as, for instance, appendicitis. In the USA, there is an incredibly complicated diagnostic handbook entitled DSM (*Diagnostic and Statistical Manual*), which lists hundreds of cognitive and mental disorders. This handbook is adapted from one edition to the next. When the third edition was published, general societal pressure had achieved that homosexuality was no longer categorised as a pathology. This decision was the greatest therapeutic success ever accomplished in history. By one stroke of the pen, millions of people were freed of their presumed disease. One must be aware, and I want to emphasise this again, that diagnoses construct realities. It should be quite clear, for example, that the mere statement that a person is schizophrenic creates a reality that can be most hermetic.

Poerksen: Could you elucidate as to what extent even the diagnosis of schizophrenia creates a reality, although there are, as it were, hard clinical criteria to support it?

Watzlawick: Let me try to illustrate this by means of an example that was brought to my attention a few years ago by the newspaper *La Nazione*. The report concerned a woman who had travelled to Grosseto from Naples, and who had to be taken to the hospital there in the state of an acute schizophrenic attack. As the small town of Grosseto did not have the adequate facilities for treatment, it was decided to send her back to Naples. The ambulance arrived, the nurses asked for the patient — and were directed to a room in which they found the woman completely dressed, with her handbag, sitting on the bed. They asked her politely to accompany them to Naples. And at this moment she apparently underwent another attack of madness, began to scream, and started to depersonalise — something that was particularly striking; depersonalisation is a typical symptom of acute schizophrenia.

Poerksen: The woman insisted that she was not the wanted patient at all?

Watzlawick: Yes — she had to be injected a sedative, was carried into the ambulance, which then drove off in the direction of Naples. Near Rome, the ambulance was stopped by the police and sent back to Grosseto. Why? The unfortunate woman was not the patient; she was an inhabitant of Grosseto, who had come to the hospital that morning to visit a relative.

Poerksen: Now this diagnostic reality obviously had no absolute validity. At some stage it was discovered that the woman was not *really* schizophrenic; at some stage — to speak with Ludwig Wittgenstein — "the facts begin to kick back".

Watzlawick: The essential point here is, however, that the confusion had created a second-order reality, in which everything the woman did was perceived as additional evidence of her madness: she resisted and defended herself, she screamed, she claimed to be someone else. What more do you need to arrive at a scientific diagnosis?

Poerksen: It seems nonetheless necessary to me to develop a language to distinguish between a person that is schizophrenic or hallucinating, and a person that is not living in such a cognitive world. Even though I share your epistemological position and agree with you in that *the one and only reality* cannot be the criterion, this undoubtedly given otherness must be amenable to articulation.

Watzlawick: The articulation of this otherness is not effectively required in any event; the only thing that has to be found is an intervention that helps; this the crucial point. When the anthropologist Gregory Bateson first came into contact with so-called mentally ill patients in a predominantly psychiatric clinic a few decades ago, he made an observation that proved to be of enormous significance for my own work. He did not ask himself — as a psychiatric perspective would suggest — in what ways the behaviour of a person corresponded with what we knew about schizophrenia. Bateson's question derived from an anthropological point of view: within which system of human relations is this behaviour meaningful? Where does it fit? And he began to invite families and relatives in order to talk to them as well as to the so-called patients. In this way, he was able to work out a representation of the system within which the apparently insane behaviour could be seen as perfectly appropriate and consistent. The behaviour in question could only be given up if the whole system was transformed in its interaction. This insight was the hour of birth of family therapy.

The loss of the Archimedean point

Poerksen: In the view of a constructivism informed by the sociology of knowledge, it cannot appear wholly convincing to restrict therapeutic procedure to families only. It has been shown that larger entities — groups, nations, and cultures — may effectively participate in the creation of potentially distressing constructions. My question is, therefore: how far should the systemic view be extended?

Watzlawick: There is no general answer to this question. If there is no progress in a therapeutic situation, one tries to enlarge the relevant system anyway, to invite other people and to make other influences visible. There are, however, practical limits.

Poerksen: Among the central premises of this form of therapy is the assumption that there is no ultimate Archimedean point that we can cling to. Perhaps a modest provocation: we might say — following Karl Kraus — that systemic-constructivist therapy is the very disease the elimination of which it claims to be. Numerous ailments arise only because people do no longer feel sheltered in the safe haven of something absolute, unquestionable, and indubitable.

Watzlawick: My only comment here is that I do not give constructivist lectures to the people who come to see me or visit my practice, nor do I engage them in profound epistemological discourses; and I would never attempt to rob anyone of their positive reality construction. That would be arrogant and dictatorial. All that is axiomatic for me is the degree of suffering.

Poerksen: However, radical scepticism with regard to the possibilities of true knowledge can — quite apart from therapeutic situations — definitely cause a sort of epistemological dizziness comparable to feeling the carpet being pulled from under one's feet. It is thought that Heinrich von Kleist took his own life as a result of the impact of Kant's criticism of knowledge.

Watzlawick: I was not aware of that. Nevertheless, I do not believe that a conclusively argued constructivist view of things will, in effect, encourage despair, as it were: all those who have learned to understand themselves as the architects of their own realities in a profound sense, will — in my view — also have acquired qualities that are in no way causes of suffering. All those who manage the breakthrough to understanding themselves as the constructors of their realities will — I believe — be deeply responsible human beings because the customary excuses — the material constraints are to blame; other people are responsible — are no longer available. They will be free; if you know that you can always change your realities you are clearly free. Furthermore, these persons will be conciliatory and tolerant; as they are aware of consciously creating and constructing their own realities, they must in due course grant others the right to do the same in their own individual ways.

Poerksen: So the consequence is: someone who implements constructivist theory as a kind of form of life, must assume self-responsibility, endure insecurity, consider change as something natural, and say farewell to the idea that the true essence of the world can be known unconditionally. Do you believe that human beings are capable of living in the constant awareness of the irrevocable imperfection and insufficiency of their existence?

Watzlawick: It would be incredibly difficult, no doubt. In my whole life, I have encountered only two people who had really progressed very far on the road to these insights. One of them was the Zen-teacher Karlfried Graf Dürkheim, who comes very close to what we call constructivist insights today in his book *Die große Befreiung [The Great Liberation]*. And the other one was Krishnamurti, whom I met personally in India. Krishnamurti was far too wise to ascend the throne erected for him by the theosophical society.

Poerksen: Both men reported experiences that we could call mystical.

Watzlawick: The question is what we mean by the word mysticism. The so-called mystical experience is something entirely indescribable. Even the label *mysticism* does not do justice to this dimension of experience. One steps wholly outside of what is given and available and experiences a kind of calmness, tranquillity, fulfilment, and harmony, which one can try to translate into the language of a religion or an ideology only after the event. As soon as one starts to describe the experience, to classify and rationalise it, one has destroyed it.

Poerksen: Whereof one cannot speak, thereof one must be silent?

Watzlawick: Yes.

About the Author

Bernhard Poerksen (b. 1969) studied German, journalism and biology, worked as a journalist, and is now junior professor of journalism and communication science at the University of Hamburg. He was awarded a Ph.D. for a thesis on the language of neo-Nazis *(Die Konstruktion von Feindbildern)*, and wrote books together with Heinz von Foerster *(Understanding Systems: Conversations on Epistemology and Ethics)* and Humberto R. Maturana *(From Being to Doing: The Origins of the Biology of Cognition)*.